Behind the
White Curtains

Behind the White Curtains

TOLA

PARTRIDGE

A Penguin Random House Company

Print information available on the last page.

To order additional copies of this book, contact
Partridge India
000 800 10062 62
orders.india@partridgepublishing.com

www.partridgepublishing.com/india

"Behind the White Curtains" which is life experience of Maya a woman. Every story has a human side. It is sure each one of you will see the glimpses of people around you in the characters that make this story. The storyteller, who suffers silently till she is brought back to the call off duty by a freak accident, will touch a cord because none of us wants to be in that situation. What extremes can one go to in order to retain control and power? What all can he let go? What are the ultimate good practices, in enlightening scenario and in human life? These are some of the questions that all conscientious people like you and me face almost on a daily basis. Maya has tried to find some answers through this story.

Maya is not a writer. It means a writer, but only by compulsion. Compulsion to express herself, compulsion to share her innermost feelings and struggles and turmoil with the larger public.

It was Sunday morning, noon just approached, end of December, world was preparing for the X'mas, people were in festive mood and were busy shopping, youngsters were planning for the New Year eve bash.

Despite the fact that it was Sunday, Dr Louis, a medical practitioner, "man with simple living and high thinking, well known for his humble, serving nature, gave the society his true services as the doctor. He was in his clinic, no patients, busy making notes of Chemistry and Physics, very meticulously, one side the pages of book which were detached from original book and on the other side, his notes based on the details provided in the book, preparing/ refreshing himself to teach his own kids who were to appear for professional entrance examination which was scheduled very shortly. He was worried as the private professional examination was a well-planned managed activity of most of the establishments, where admission to talented deserving students had very meager opportunity. The students who were blessed by divinity and the influential parents were certain about their admission to the Professional Studies. He as a parent too was blessed by divinity and was not an influential person. He was dependent only on the establishment where the entrance examination was conducted by the authority, where the chances of managing the list were nil.

Suddenly a lady rushed in his clinic. She had injury on her head, feet and blood was oozing. Her dress was torn and she was trying to cover it with her off-white and green slash, her long silky hair rolled on her shoulders. She uttered only one word doctor and just tried to sit down on the patient chair and she sunk down. Dr Louis got frightened, pat her on her cheeks, which were filth," Maya Maya Maya! Get up!!! What's wrong with you? No answer, he checked her pulse, which was very low, hurriedly he lifted her and put her straight on table.

Maya opened her eyes and tears rolled down on her cheeks, Dr. Louis smiled, and said "You scarred me". How did you reach here with so many injuries. She acclaims and said I met with an accident, but I am fine. Dr Louis lost his temper, how can you say this, you are badly injured. She mar-mars, first see on my head is there an injury. Without wasting a single second, he started cleaning her wounds. She said there is lot of pain at the lower back and she could not get up. He told her I am seeing brave mother in this condition first time, have you kept that award which you won two years back. She said of course doctor. I know you must have; that was the biggest award in your life.

The doctor cleaned her wounds, which were about 10-12 in number. Her right leg by then swollen up, he puts medicine and took X"rays to ensure that there is no fracture. After few minutes he said no fracture, she sacrificially smiles and said she knew this.

After giving her injection and treatment, he said "speak "; what happened, she laughed and said that she was riding two wheeler, going to market and suddenly the vehicle skid and person on another two wheeler; just behind her with the vehicle ran over her. Doctor was in a slightly irritated mood said; why you have to use two wheeler, when you have four wheeler. She smiled and said; she was very sure that one day she will be rich enough to go to market in four wheeler and get vegetable from air-conditioned vegetable mall.

Maya after a while used her mobile and called her so called daughter cum student Shaba, and informed her; that she has just met with accident and now in Dr. Louis's clinic, and asked her to bring shawl. Shaba got anxious/nervous, she hired a rickshaw and reached Dr. Louis's clinic, where she saw her memsahib was in a pathetic condition. She hugged her and both of them travelled back home in private vehicle. The mechanic, who brought two wheeler, was waiting for Maya to arrive, his favourite lady in the lane, who use to smile always and whenever she passed from his small repair Tapri and greeted with happy voice "How are you Lore, What is happening". He parked her two wheeler, she thanked Lore and asked Shaba to give him his fees, he thanked her and said If you need any help please donot forget me? If She said ho yes sure I will.

After reaching home her so called hut (paradise), she spoke to herself I am fine; got into the very baggy shirt and skirt, hit directly to bed. After resting for few hours Maya was thinking about when floodgates were opened to private scholastic players, recognizing opportunity at the right time, how royal man jumped in to liberalize scholastic! How slowly he converted it to his kingdom of his own. By adding more institutes, schools, making Maya work 12 hours a day and finally to manage all, his family members were in system. By then doctor was at Maya's residence and was quietly listening to Maya:

Maya said: You know what would be the end of story

Doctor said No, how I would know: she said at the end the progress report of higher learning would be excellent and would be projected as world class learning.

Dr Louis warned her not to go to work and take complete bed rest atleast for a fortnight. Maya smiled and said; tomorrow she is required to go to work, as many of staff members were on leave and her entire team members were transferred, time bound tasks were to be completed. Dr Louis said, you donot behave like a doctor, though he knew she could treat herself, the establishment will not be closed if she does not go to office for few days.

Dr Louis thought for a moment that "True education is realized by what one internalizes and Maya's education has been through school of hard knocks!

She worked hard with positive outlook and always willing to help everyone! It was this attribute which made her truly educated good human being.

Suddenly Maya changed the topic and said that, but you tell me why you were writing notes, when I entered to your clinic.

The doctor said these days; establishment has become only money making machines. My both the kids, are preparing for an entrance examination, Maya can you believe, the teachers /staff are not even qualified to teach them, she said why? how it can be? He said many of the staff members are relatives/acquaints of the royal man and his family. She said that is the problem in almost all the private organization, it is a family business. On many occasions, we are helpless, though we work with all the honesty, sincerity which is never been considered. He said: Maya, you are working more than 30 years nearly, you know better. She said yes.

Actually Dr Louis wanted to be with her for some time, as first time he noticed that Maya was stressed, under tension, because of which she is suffering, but doesnot want to disclose her agony, fear, her uncertainty, helplessness to anyone.

He wanted her to speak out heart, since he has seen her last so many years, working hard, marching ahead with courage, positive attitude, though many of academicians felt that Maya always had attitude of "teaching lesson to others", how wrong they are, they donot know what Maya has faced in real life. He has never ever seen her in tension, pressure. This was the first time he has seen Maya under tension.

He encouraged her to speak, she said: you know doctor, I am not an academician and that too do not hold a Research Notch, but doctor, much better than so called an academician.

He said why you are sounding so low on this, has anybody told you,

She said yes, on many occasions in my working hours, but every time I have argued and proved my views that administrators are not less, they have experience in both academics as well as administration. A good academician may not be good administrator but a good administrator can be good academician. Doctor said you are right (he did not know whether she was right or wrong, but wanted her to speak).

The Dr Louis gave endurance hearing to Maya, he was astonish to hear the suffering, harassment, insult, which Maya has under gone through out. He wanted to share with his kids so that they would be more somber in their studies and works hard to get free seat through authority entrance examination rather than managed entrance examination.

After big pause, the story continued

Maya devoted prime 20 years of her life for this establishment. Very closely she witnessed rapid downfall of ethics and educational standards. The establishment (where she was earning her bread), was offering the Professional Studies for the students who were admitted to undergraduate, postgraduate and research studies The establishment was approved. But the said establishment was under a public trust, which was headed by a royal man and other trustees.

The establishment at the beginning had strictly followed the norms, guidelines', rules and regulations, but as the years passes by, the trust was successful in their research of dilution of rules and regulations. The trust was led by royal man (deep water fish) commonly known as "royal man with many feathers in his cap" and other trustees and other family members including their pause sisters, nephews, nieces, friends, among them was "Vice- Commander" who was more powerful, wicked-witch, who had shallow knowledge of the higher learning system and administration. The vice-commander (chief Executive of Management) had good networking with all the political leaders, persons of repute. All the other so called trustee were commonly known as "tiny tot " were, "devils of third category" The trust was responsible for appointing a chief, who was supposed to be CEO of the establishment and who was supposed to be an man of repute, scholar. The position of chief was very important position and was directly reporting to "royal man". The royal man was also the first man of the establishment. He was the king of his own created kingdom. The royal man had worked very hard, in the initial stages, and with help of rich, helping nature, reputed personalities of the city started one establishment and as the business flourished, slowly and steadily established many more establishments and finally got rid of all those who have helped in creating empire and he became from Sage to royal man. The term of then chief was coming to an end. The process of selecting the new chief started, at the same time Maya's immediate boss also had relinquish the post and she dedicatedly performed his duties too.

After completing the required formalities, the d'day had come where the management was to select the new chief. She said purposely management because, it was all managed selection process. Maya was specially called and informed that selection of new chief has already been done and the chairman of committee has already appreciated as he is the man of repute, academician, scientist who will take the establishment to greater height.

She obeyed orders, thinking that authorities are wiser and must have followed the norms, because generally new chief appointment is being made after due deliberations, search, keeping in mind the vision, and reputation of the establishment.

Everybody was on high alert, the staff members were told that the new proposed chief is very strict, scientist, does not talk much, short tempered person, follows protocols and rules. The staff was already very panic and was cursing the management for thinking of brings such a "Kudus" person, but they did not have choice.

The committee consist eminent academicians, persons of repute, arrived for the interview. The then chief was in his office, she was instructed by the management and was directed to be present and arrange the selection procedure. The old chief was upset, but she had no alternative but to follow the directives and procedure of selection of new chief.

The process of selection began, few academicians, scientists have shown interest to become chief. She and her staff were anxious to see the proposed, incoming chief. Each candidate was provided vehicle to come to the venue. One by one they arrived, and finally the hero (that day they all were anxious to see hero), jokingly her subordinates were saying, what mischief she would do. The mischievous lot "disciples" had put gum (sticking solution) on one of the sofas, where the hero was to be made to sit, and Maya's class four employees were smiling at her.

Finally hero arrived; one of her colleagues informed and pointed out that he was the hero. She welcomed him to the establishment and made him sit and thought he will never be able to get up because of sticking solution. But he was lucky, the moment he was about sit he saw a known person and he greeted some other candidate and there were exchange of views among themselves and they occupied another sofa. Her colleagues were in mood of fun and hilarity, she became quite sad, thinking he has won the first stroke but thought that she must behave herself and stop doing mischief. Actually Maya had analyzed his personality as very simple, straight forward and to-the-point professor and teacher by heart. And her disciple said hope your fortune Teller, prophecy is correct.

The hero went inside to appear for an interview, the vice-commander, who was also the one of the important trustees, who was second in command after royal man and also related to royal man. The vice-commander had very good contact with the ministers and hold over the national capital authorities. The vice-commander called Maya and instructed her after he finishes interview, just take him for lunch to guest house. She got second chance to do some mischief, but immediately she was assigned some other responsibility. She said "Man proposes God disposes", one of her very witty assistant said "he will look at you all if he get appointed.

She laughingly told him; he has to work with the naughty team and since he is very serious type of person, he probably doesnot know how to smile, laugh and enjoy working with children like us. All scientists are same, but he resemble with Gautam Budha, she was muttering to herself hope he smile and work and enjoy working with the office, we are expert in our territory and teach people to enjoy work.

The selection procedure was over, the committee, the members had their lunch, and the selection committee's report was sealed in an envelope, which she was to place it before the royal man. The hero was taking lot of time to have lunch, she was getting irritated, he has come interview or has come to enjoy lunch coolly. Finally he came from guest house; he was drove to the royal man. Her vehicle carrying the report was followed by hero's vehicle and also vice-commander was in another car it was as if carnival of the President.

After reaching to another office the hero was given VIP treatment, Maya placed the report before the royal man; he asked her did she get the opportunity to meet him. She shook her head and said no. All praise worthy words was spoken about him. Thinking in her mind really the great person is coming to establishment.

The hero was called by the royal man, after half hour discussion/interview, the hero came out. She asked him, what time is your flight to Off-centre or shall we make your stay arrangement. A strict voice replied, I have my own arrangements. By appearance the hero was like refined, clear-headed, down to earth person, but we were to experience the same said Maya to one of her assistant who had accompanied her. "

She return back to office, leaving the hero who was in mustard color blazer, with black codraw trousers, thinking he to be real hero what way God alone knows.

Her staff was waiting for her running commentary about new hero.

Maya spent about one hour, doing mimicry and was joined by her disciples.

She was informed by the Management that new chief would soon take over and likely visit the campus on Saturday, which was the only day when they had holiday and were in relax mood, since last two years only work, work and work which has made the jack dull. But they were told that the new chief will not interact with anyone of them or even meet them. Maya could feel the happiness and joy on the faces of her staff which was beyond description.

We were relax, but suddenly the HR Head entered her office, he was another crook, cunning, deceitful who had conveniently, fraudulently had appointed many of his relatives in the establishment and all of them were the members of 'tiny tot team' and were misreporting to him and further he use to misreport to royal man and vice-commander. Their behviour was like a bug that keeps biting the people and survive by sucking the blood. His personality was like a low grade person, uncultured, corrupt, had milt money by unethical ways within short spin of time he had purchased a three star hotel and that was his side income. He being HR chief, who was no role to play in the establishment's affairs, but had all the powers. Though did not know the systems in the higher learning but could manage the affairs. In last so many years, not more than six months any qualified executive could work under him. He never likes, or never ever shares any information, official information with anyone. On many occasions in his absence the vice-commander, the legal advisor has faced problems and ultimately Maya has to come to the rescue of the establishment on HR matters. He requested Maya to provide a system, he needs some print outs. She helped him. After taking few print outs he vanished and after few minutes Maya was called to guest house, as the new chief has arrived to guest house. She thought, his new office would be in the guest house instead of establishment, because on the day of the interview also he took quite some time to come to office. Maya reached the guest house, the new chief was again the mustard colour blezare, After greeting him officially, she was introduced to him. The vice-commander spoke very high about her. The Hero smiled. Maya was instructed to sign some papers for new chief and also obtain his signature too. She placed the papers before him, he immediately started signing, and she requested him: Sir; please read the papers and if you agree then only you sign. he smiled and said I trust you.

She got his first teaching put up the papers which are perfect in order, correct, as per rules and trust the colleagues His one sentence, made her to change views about the hero. After the signature, Maya was lost in thoughts, thinking how a person can trust her without even having working experience with her, is he a professional or like previous chief?.

She did not wanted to think more about the hero, because according to her opinion all men are of same category selfish, think about them first unlike woman who always think for other first and then for herself. He would soon start behaving like previous chief.

Her inner-self voiced that she was to be proven wrong very soon.

Being Administrative Head of the establishment she was given the responsibility of welcoming the new chief. As usual she was very busy completing the documents, a brief about the establishment, the progress, his office and what not. The new chief arrived on the day when he was to take over the charge from the old chief.

The old chief, who was from professional background, a clumsy person, knife, but dangerous, use to believe in gossiping more than work. Never believed in innovation, research and was not in good terms with vice-commander. Most of the staff members were not comfortable working or interacting with him, as he was short tempered person too. He arrived early as planned and the staff members were ready with the formalities and at the same time the old chief was not ready to meet the staff or address them, Maya had perused the old chief to address, give his last message to the staff, in his last addressed he mentioned Maya as darling of the establishment, she was shocked, the person day in and night argue, kept the chief very busy and did not allowed him to approve which was not in favour of the establishment, how suddenly became his darling, Anker of the establishment. He admitted that he use to always admire her work, but did not wanted to mention or appreciate it, otherwise make her feel proud of herself. He acknowledged that she was the person who has really worked hard, intelligently and helped in expansion, of the establishment.

The new chief arrived with the vice-commander, both of them exchanged some official papers; the then chief was received by his son and left the office.

The vice-commander and Maya accompanied him to his new office, briefed him about what are official papers kept for his perusal and also briefed him about the procedure, rules and regulations. Not a word of appreciation, only one word "Hmm". The vice-commander said good job. Immediately after was introduction of officers with the new chief, everbody introduced themselves. When her turn came, the New chief said I know about you. Maya was upset, but had no choice.

The whole process was running out of time, he was to visit the departments of the establishments, he said he had appointment with royal man and he doesnot like to be late and never was late when he has appointment. **The second teaching/commandment from Hero to be punctual, time is precious and he believes in timely work.**

She thought, it is nice way the new chief is communicating to them, what he believe and practice.

She immediately noted in her diary, his two teaching in two days. But was really impressed by him, the way he was communicating his principles.

The new chief left for the day, her so called children (her assistants) were waiting for her to have discussion about new chief and do some masti, tingal, regarding the new chief. They were soon disappointed, as their leader was bit serious. All of them asked; what is the matter, she told them, the new chief probably has scanned us thoroughly, he knows that we are very witty, mischievous lot with whom he has to work and control us.

The chief started attending office, he used to be present before all of us and leave the office after everyone. **This was third teaching/directives to her that as second position in the organization should reach to office before the staff comes in and devote more time.** She was thinking, she already work nearly 10 hours a day, what he expect from her 12 hours a day. She thought of talking to him next day, as she entered his office, and greeted him, he said yes; you may start coming at 9.15a.m. every day will have morning briefing and then start the work, you may leave office when I leave, or whatever time you finish your work.

Three days, three teachings, slowly he started controlling the establishment affairs. She was wondering with new chief another new boss, "we are in greater trouble than before". She thought of sharing her thoughts with children (team) during their laughing session, which was scheduled every day after the office hours for 15-20 minutes, before the staff is to disburse for the day.

That evening, she shared his three teachings in three days.

Her witty assistant said "I told you all before only once he comes on Board he will take care of you all" ".from that day we kept chief's pat name as "Baba". The laughing session was over, after completing the day's task, she started at 8p.m. for home, but on her way she was thinking about baba. The question which was worrying her was, the moment she use to enter his office, he use to give directives for the question which Maya was yet to put to him. How does he know what is there in her after mind?. But believe it doctor; still Maya said was not able to get the answer. Doctor said; why you donot ask him. She said; let me complete research myself.

The chief was strict was giving impression of "Gautam Budha", every day one file was to be placed before him. She remembers there was Management Council meeting in the same month of his joining. She put the draft agenda to him for approval, he made 29 corrections, she lost her patience, she was in angry mood went to him, as usual before she could say anything, he said, I know previously in this establishment, the style of agenda is the same what you have put up to me as the draft based on previous agenda. But improvement and change is always good and we should happily accept it. She had no words; he called for a cup of tea as it was tea time. After having tea, she left his office and requested him to wait for few minutes, so that he can approve the corrected agenda. While walking towards **her** office, **it was his**

fourth teaching/commandment; change is always good which leads to improvement.

Maya was getting lost, as to what kind of person he is, never laughs, whole day keeps working, without wasting a single minute.

Her witty assistant during our laughing session said Madam he is much more clever and well versed with the system, *"He is far advance than you and me".*

It was last week of April, first month of chief, She placed before him the new regulations sent by the authority. Also briefed him that we need to issue a notification regarding revised qualifications as stipulated in the regulations so that appointments procedure could be initiated immediately. His question was has Management Council accepted it if yes why you are waiting. The notification was drafted made ready and was placed before the chief on 24th April, he went through the same and that was the first notification the new chief has approved and signed.

Maya decided not to give up, if he knows rules and regulations than she was not less. She started speaking very official language with him and to the point reply to everything that he would ask. After two three days, probably he realized that Maya was not in her usual cheerful mood. During the next morning session, he said; we have to work together very hard to make this establishment as world class and have to work hard to make it as highest grade establishment. I alone cannot do, it is possible only if you extend your full support and so as leadership team of the establishment. With this attitude, we will able achieve our goal faster than stipulated time. **That was his fifth teaching, work as a team by supporting each other and achieve the goal.**

On the day of Management Council meeting, when she went with the papers to placed it before him there were some mistakes, he pointed out, was little upset with Maya, Maya was very simple person and was down to earth, she immediately submitted her apology and assured him that will correct the same before the meeting and not let him down. He said I am happy with you;

I like people who accept their mistake and donot give justification and ready to correct the mistake. **That was his sixth teaching/commandment, accept the mistake and correct it.**

The first meeting of chief went off very well, the chief was happy, Maya had already informed him that it was her first meeting as the secretary wanted his support. He assured her and really she was totally dependent on him, after the meeting he and the vice-commander congratulated Maya for conducting meeting well. But the chief made his impression; he briefed the members about his idea of taking the establishment to greater height. He spoke about research, publications and how to enhance the branding of the establishment. As a researcher, he emphasized to undertake challenging ventures, even failures in projects takes to new heights. He emphasized to undertake more work than capacity, that expands our limits and when we introspect, we feel that we have gained new skills and capacities. He really empowered the students and staff at large.

Maya requested him to expedite the matter of appointment of the officer who would supervise her work, as it was vacant for last three months. He promised her that he would take care of the same and appoint the officer on priority with following all the rules, procedures. Maya was more than happy.

After a week of the meeting, the draft minutes were placed before Baba (chief), the style was the same which was followed for years together. He during his morning session, asked her to send the soft copy to him. She immediately obeyed his directives, but was wondering what he is going to do. Late evening she received the correct copy with corrections and it was mentioned **"word is an important tool"** use it very carefully. **This was his seventh teaching/commandment**. She went through the corrected minutes, was very happy as she did not agree with his two inputs. Next morning during their morning briefing session, as soon as she entered his office and before she could utter the word he said; are there any suggestions from you.

She was shocked, how does he knows, what she has placed before him the suggestions and first time in one month's time Baba agreed. She was thrilled. The vice-commander was also very happy that chief is getting adjusted to new environment and he is getting good support from all the staff.

As per the procedure, a meeting was scheduled with all the leadership team, The leadership team was another unique team, mixture of many fold people, with different nature, culture, all of them were enjoying their freedom in respect to academics, some of them were really genius, scholarly person, but their hand and legs were tied so that they are controlled by the vice-commander. But they were very faithfully to the vice-commander; daily report was their unforgettable task, though officially they were to report to the chief. They believed in divided we stand and divided we fall concept. The habit of following autonomous culture, freedom, was difficult to break through. The monthly meeting was gaining momentum and importance because of the chief, his approach, participatory governance system. The chief was clear and transparent, would place all the policy matters before the leadership team and for him views, suggestions, dissent from each one of them was very important. Maya was instructed to strictly follow the order regarding agenda of the meeting and how to conduct the meeting, no matters to be discussed other than agenda points.

As usual, before the meeting she went with the papers to him this time chief was happy and he complimented her that she have followed all the instructions.

She went to his office just 10 minutes before the meeting so that we could start the meeting on time, Maya reminded him, exactly five minutes before he got up from his chair and walked to the venue where the meeting was scheduled. The leadership team was just parking themselves for the meeting. The chief read the thought for the day which was displayed on the screen he occupied the chair looked at the clock and instructed her to start the meeting. Everybody was little taken a back because few of the members were yet to join.

Before she could start the agenda item, he said; if you all wish to greet me when I enter the meeting room than it should be done in one style, not that some of you stand and some you are sitting. I have no issue, if you all donot get up and wish me. Further he mentioned that all the meetings where he is in the chair will start in time and will conclude in time.

To start any work in time and conclude in time, secondly as per the traditions, when guru/teacher enters the class or a meeting, as mark of respect, members have to stand together and greet the chief or guru. **This was his eighth teaching. Maya said, Believe** me I was really getting lost with his style of working, but didn't dare to ask any questions, information.

The vice-commander, after the meeting asked Maya about the new chief, her reply was he is too good, very professional and we are learning a lot from him. She too was very happy. She told me the organisation wanted a dynamic leader. Maya again on the same day reminded her regarding appointment of an officer which was pending.

During early days of June month, there was sudden meeting, where Maya was called to attend, the vice-commander and royal man were present. She entered the meeting room; the chief looked at her in usual angry style. Maya was wondering what for is this meeting. The royal man smiled at Maya and said we are starting a new programme and none better than you can do it within 20 days' time period as you are expert in launching the new programmes. Maya was given complete details about the programme and was informed the name of the person (academician) who would lead the new establishment with new programme. He said, you are given 10 days to complete the task and place before me the draft proposal.

After the meeting she left the meeting room and was murmuring, how to make this miracle happen?, give details regarding starting a new programme in ten days, "Bap ka Raj hai keya" Last four years Maya was only doing this work, making proposal starting new institutes, facing committees and now this new chief (Baba) also started ordering her. They should appoint the officer immediately, with just addition of small perk, which she was not prepared to do work of two officers, double duty.

During her briefing with her staff in the next morning, she placed before them the directives of the Management and also expressed her anger, her witty assistant said" Madam, *donot tell anything, you will work hard and all the credits will be given to someone else* " donot be sweet and impress us. Probably or he was absolutely right, as per her psychology, she use to always react first and after sometime complete the task efficiently and get it implemented.

Maya started working on the proposal incorporating financial, academic, administrative, infrastructure viability and the proposal was ready to be placed before the chief within four working days. She discussed the same with **her** team, again **her** witty assistant said *"Please read carefully, otherwise chief will take your class"* He was right, all of us went through the complete proposal that morning she did not meet the chief in the morning for briefing. He called his secretary, who was one of the member tiny tot, he was very good in misreporting to vice-commander, at the same time cunningly use to take care of secretariat. He was good in the logistic arrangements but did not have the communication skills. He was rich person. He was also one of the committee members of organization allocation. The chief asked whether Maya have come or not, and if on leave, whether he has granted permission of leave of absence.

The secretary immediately replied: Mam never takes leave; she is in the office from 7a.m. onwards. He asked him why? What is the matter? He had no reply, because he knew if some proposal was to be prepared then the team will not see the time and madam will come early to finish her daily administrative work so that everything will be functioning smoothly.

The chief got up from his chair, the Secretary asked him are you having some meeting, he replied "NO". I am going to the madam's office, the Secretary was trying to accompany him, he stopped him and said *(you do your work)*. Her team was working at their respective work stations; Maya was engrossed, working typing and referring to some material. The chief entered her office, her team was surprised but they just stood up as mark of respect to chief, he nodded his head and speedily entered her office, she did not realize the chief has come in. The moment she noticed him, it was centre shock for her. The words were not coming out of her mouth. He could feel she shocked to see him, he sat on chair, she was still standing, he said sit sit. He asked: what was she doing since morning. Maya showed him the draft proposal which is ready within four working days and not ten days. There was still question mark on his face. she could read, he said; one should follow the procedure and when somebody sends email that means it has to be replied immediately, of course where there is administrative procedure one should comply within three working days. All this was going bumper over her head, as she did not want anyone to be disturbed her, as was to complete the task given to her. He was waiting for her reply. She said yes sir. He said implement. He walked *out of her office. After he left her office, all her assistants rushed to her room and asked "what happened madam"? she said nothing but still she did not paid much attention to his visit to her office.*

After few hours, her assistant rushed and said there was a mail from chief, complementing you, which was sent in the morning at 8a.m. and all of us were so busy with the new initiative that we have not seen your mail box. Maya said let us not get distracted by his compliments, let us finished our work. Late in the afternoon, he asked his secretary again, *If Madam has finished the work , please call her , I have some important work."* The secretary immediately informed her to come to his office. Maya had completed the proposal and draft print was placed before him. He laughed first time after his joining; he said I have yet to see a person like you so dedicated. She submitted her apology for not reporting to him during the morning briefing session. He accepted the same. He said, email means there is communication which requires your immediate attention; it is fast mode of communication in the technology savvy world. The mails are to be replied immediately, she said we, everyday only today we have not checked.

To reply the mails immediately atleast acknowledged them, decision to be communicated within three working days. The procedure what he has laid down to be followed meticulously, no deviation. **This was his ninth teaching/ commandment.**

After handing over the draft to him, Maya rushed to her office, to check what are the e-mails about which he is so concerned. By then her assistant has taken out the prints of emails so that procedure could be followed of replying them.

She was happy that he acknowledged our work through a mail. We shared among ourselves his compliments. Maya immediately thanked him for compliments. In the mid of June, he informed her that another new programme to be started in different discipline and a new professor who would lead the programme and institute has already been identified.

Maya was not surprised because in their establishment, this was normal activity to start a programme within few days.

The chief approved the draft prepared by Maya for launching the new programme with some minor inputs. He discussed the same with the vice-commander and royal man. The programme was advertised; the chief and vice-commander called for a press conference and declared the programme to be started from July/August.

Meanwhile there was a meeting scheduled with the academic committee of the establishment, the position of two members were vacant, Maya placed before the chief the constitution of committee as the notice for the scheduled meeting was to be sent. He was so fast in nominating eminent academicians; she was surprised as they were waiting for his invitation. He spoke to the vice-commander, both of them unanimously agreed to nominate the persons. He asked Maya to send them letter of invitation. She got approved draft invitation from him because wanted to know his style of writing. While approving the draft, he added few lines. He smiled and said, you wanted to know **my** way of writing, otherwise you could have sent the communication as per official previous records. Again **her** research started as to how he knows what she was thinking, which still not completed or come to a conclusion.

The chief was a researcher and visionary, one day he asked her about the display of details of the establishment. Maya started thinking, whether something has gone wrong as nothing was there on the lousy display of details. How you will communicate to world, students, academic fraternity that what you are doing. First time she replied rightly to him, through display of details. Then he said what you are waiting for, revamp the website. Maya said how, she have no powers to do there is a communication officer, who is ought to do and not she. He like her frank opinion, he said everybody should be accountable for their work. **Accountability is absolutely mandatory was his tenth teaching/commandment.**

The communication officer was summoned to his office, the officer said we have been trying to upgrade the website but it is taking some time and in near future it will be completed. He called on Maya, he said both of you complete this task before he come back from an international conference which was end of July. She requested him to connect them to vendor, who is creative, has past experience to designing a website and also who will not quote a very high financial estimate. To our surprise, the vendor was identified and was called for a meeting with all officers of the establishments. All of them had meeting along with the chief and the vendor and chief instructed all to give inputs and inputs to be approved by Maya as she was the senior most person in the establishment. Everybody agreed to the directives and started working. The deadline was given to everyone. The communication officer was requested to be more responsible and give his best and not to put burden on her shoulder.

The chief asked her, whether she was aware of new rules sent by the authority. Maya replied yes and just reminded him that in the month of April, she has placed before him. He questioned her again have we reconstituted all the Boards as per the new rules, her answer was yet to be done. He said why are we waiting for, she was quite, he again asked what is the hitch, very positively she said we were waiting for you to join so that we can reconstitute. He laughed and said people may come and go but the establishment has to function it should not stop working; it should not be person dependable. **Nobody is indispensable; our system should be so transparent and accurate that all the team should be able to work even if one person is not there. This was his eleventh teaching/commandment.**

From that day onwards, her entire team had complete access to all the data, her email was shared with all of them, and believe it there was friendly positive vibes in the air of the establishment, which was felt by each one and even was felt by the outsiders.

The chief had already discussed with the vice-commander, which she did not know. He said keep all the administrative procedures ready and on his return from conference. But as usual, her principle not to keep the matter pending, next morning all the papers duly completed administratively were placed before him, he was astonished, he went to meet royal man and requested him to nominate the person on his behalf on the boards as per the new regulations. That was first week of July. The wheels of the establishment were moving very fast in the positive direction. He was receiving lot of appreciations from the organization.

The staff at the establishment was so busy with the new directives that there was hardly any time to think of anything else. It was joint efforts of each of the employee to take the establishment to greater height.

It was Tuesday, it was around 12 noon, Maya went with some important papers to him and suddenly saw on fair lady sitting on the sofa with the architect, the architect knew her as he has completed the work of establishment office. The chief introduced her to that incoming leader/champion who would lead the new programme. She smiled and greeted her and welcomed her on Board. Maya finished her work and was back in the office and informed her children (disciples) that new leader is joining us shortly. Her witty assistant said *"let the disciple come we will see her "*. She told him the new incoming leader is Baba's pet, be careful, she looks like a serious person.

On the 10th July the chief asked her is there any process to send the progress of the establishment to royal man. She again reminded him that last two months she was placing the report of the establishment on every 6th of month, but he was not happy with the presentation or the language of the report in which it was to be placed before the royal man. He said please send me draft report and also the previous report submitted then. He said I will work on it on Sunday. She was thinking why he is following her footsteps of working on Sunday. But did not bother much, because his x'ray eyes would read what is going in her mind because on many occasion when she did not agree with his decision and use to think before him about the same, he use to immediately ask her as why she not agreeing to him and some time he use to modify his decision but never changed it.

On Monday morning during their morning briefing the chief gave her the report which was to be submitted to royal man and instructed that now onwards in this style we will submit the report quarterly not only to royal man but also to all the board members, leadership team and all the officer of the establishment. Maya asked him why you want me to go through the report, you as the chief must have completed very accurately. He said, it always better to share the reports because you may get good inputs and people will feel that they are involved in the activities of the establishment and sharing with your own trustworthy people is always good. **He said feeling of involvement is very important when you are working in the organization. This was his twelveth teaching/commandment.**

Maya was really getting lost but at the back of mind, always thinking that is he trying to teach her a lesson for the mischief, she did during his interview and he has come to know about it. This fear was there. But as usual hardly any time to think other than work.

She received appointment order for the new champion/leader regarding starting of another new programme/establishment; it was of the same field of our Baba.

The leader/champion went to meet the chief and he directed her to me to receive the order and get the brief about the administrative procedure to be followed. That day the secretary was on leave and her witty assistant was locum for secretary. The new champion/leader started walking towards her office and suddenly there was a call from chief office, *"Jumbo Jet" is reaching to you be careful, she asked him who this, he said "You see yourself now"* And soon the new champion was in her office, she handed over the appointment order, after reading the champion, was very upset and all the anger was on Maya. She offered a glass of water and requested her to let her know what the problem is and probably she will be able to help out. The leader pointed out the corrections required to be done in the order, she immediately informed the HR Head and requested for the correction, a special messenger was sent to collect the corrected copy. The corrected copy was handed over to the leader.

She was little settled and Maya requested one of her assistant to take her and introduced to the staff and further to her new office where she was provided with temporary arrangement, till her new institute is ready. Maya did not know that she was a scientist till chief informed her. He further mentioned that the new school will be inaugurated soon after his return and requested to give full support and help to the leader for establishing the same. But the new champion was not friendly person, was busy getting work done for labs and other details for new institute.

The new boards were formed and invitations were accepted by the members of eminence. The chief informed her that he and two other members from the management would take a trip to USA in the third week of July. Her thinking was right, this was first coin of the organization to capture the new chief so that he is under obligation. But since they were child hood friends so chief would be safe and will not follow into their prey.

The chief started attending conferences, giving lectures, writing articles and whatnot. On one occasion while returning from the meeting or from the airport, the driver reached late to receive him and chief lost his cool, immediately he called her and said you being officer incharge and directly reporting me should check with the lower officer; whether the arrangements for me has been made or not. From that day onward, Maya started ensuring with the chief, whenever he was travelling regarding the arrangement without fail.

During the third week, the interviews for another officer ranked above were held; Maya too had applied for the same with the recommendation of former chief. She appeared for the interview, the chief was the chairman and other members were little known to her but did not bother to meet anyone because of firm believe that if she have to get the position it should on her merit and not through any pressure.

Her witty assistant said "You will get the post on your merit, you donot need to request any one's to recommendations" The interview went off well one of the member said that she should be as the panel member because of her vast experience. There was no communication from HR department, she understood someone else has been selected and was happily waiting for the new champion. The next day, the chief was to leave for conference at national level and further another one at international level. While leaving he informed that he would be available on **emails only and try to be independent and work and take the decision wherever required and he will stand by the decision. This was his thirteenth teaching/commandment.**

On the day of his departure, the one of the relative of royal man visited the chief, who was pursuing research for last three years and there was no communication from the establishment to her, as usual the being royal man's relative, was in very angry mood and was complaining to the chief. Maya's was called by the chief and asked for the details and progress of the case. But she did not knew the status of candidate case. The chief was not in mood to listen to her, she was feeling humiliated, but as per the protocol, procedure, she did not want to argue and submit her clarification before the relative. Soon she got the details from the concerned department and placed it before the chief. He was upset as the document and the procedure was not followed and due which the establishment would have been in trouble. Maya by then knew and could read his expression, she immediately corrected the documents and prepared the documents and the chief as a very special case approved. After the royal man's relative left, the chief asked for explanation for such kind of delay, irregularities in the research wing. But unfortunately the then responsible officers were transferred from the department and left the department in unfinished, unethical manner the then chief did not bother to correct the documents and look into the matter legally. The chief was put into fix and had no choice to accept and oblige the relative of royal man. The relative was very happy and managed to complete the thesis and finally submitted and for final approval. The royal man has already spoken to the external juries and finally the managed research work was accepted though the chief did not accept the recommendation. Maya was asked to sign the documents by the vice-commander and the royal man. A grand party was organized and the chief and Maya were also invited for the same. The personal assistant of the management was one of the stout who was expert in forging the documents, writing of other and could manage the work well. He was appointed for his ethical expertise and was one of the important members from the tiny tots team. Her witty assistant said:

Madam, He has strings to pull all over so be careful, he is beyond imagination.

The chief left for the conference in the afternoon, but he has left good amount of home work for her. The staff was little relaxed but not she. He wanted daily report and updates through an email, so that he knows what is happening behind him and whether all of them really working. This was our testing period and did not want to fail. Though the chief was not there everybody was working with full zeal. The royal man called her on the same evening and asked her whether everything is fine at the establishment and Maya decided to report to him every day the happening at the establishment and send an email to chief.

Maya started reporting to royal man every day at 7 p.m. and before leaving the office updates was sent to chief. The Management was happy with chief and his style of working. When the chief was away, the royal man informed her that inauguration of new programme and the institute would be second week of August and necessary procedure to be followed and make the arrangements. Her team was not surprised because they were used to this kind of emergency. The new appointed leader was little apprehensive about the opening of institute, but Maya was very positive as in past they had such situation many times. She started moving the wheels faster than expected the new champion/leader was wondering, what Maya is up too, did not bother about anybody because to avoid embarrassment last minute which the new leader was not able to understand. The Champion stopped talking to her because with her status she used to be on 7th floor (up in the sky) and Maya being a poor worker was at the bottom of the building. Her aim was very clear that the institute has to start functioning from 2nd week of August as per orders. The deadlines were given to all the vendors the chief projects was very kind enough and extended full cooperation as we have done many projects together. But without fail her reporting was to the chief and royal man.

Maya was busy with many deadlines, the day chief was to arrive, that day she left office at 12mid night. The chief was to arrive, at 2a.m. she text the chief, whether all arrangements are in place? He was happy and at the same time he felt she was obeying his instructions. He shared this incidence with the vice-commander. They were pleased with her working.

The chief was in the office by 9a.m., Maya placed all the papers which required his decision/directions. The chief looked very tired, but did not say anything. He said he will leave the office little early. Each department head one by one briefed the chief and updated him with their work. The chief was satisfied. She was little taken a back; the chief did not bring chocolates for them, thought what a stingy chief. He has not yet given joining party and now not a single sweet. But felt that at the right time she will convey him the message.

The chief received appreciation from the royal man stated that the establishment is fortunate to have him as the chief though he deserve to the chief of reputed establishment. His experience and expertise in teaching, research and innovation were enviable. He was succeeded in bringing stalwarts in research on the campus of the establishment. He has given impetus to star new programmes. The staff starting respecting his administrative skills, decision making ability and his erudition. Further appreciated that he could be his national and international contact at the door step of the establishment.

The chief was on the top of the world. Her witty assistant said*: chief has passed with distinction marks and madam has already predicted but who is going to bell the cat?*

The chief instructed her to draft a format and also terms and conditions, as he proposed to recognize some research centres attached to the establishment so that research will progress and it will benefit both the organizations. The format and communication/instructions in draft form were placed before him. The first time in one stroke the chief approved the same.

The new website was ready as per directives of the chief and was waiting for his approval to upload the same. After discussion the chief approved the same and within 24 hours the new vibrant, people friendly website was uploaded.

The chief was in teaching mood, he told his secretary with good intention to enhance is education so that he can get promotion. But the secretary did not take his advice in right spirit. He informed the vice-commander and not the right thoughts behind the chief's advice. After few days, the secretary was promoted as the officer of the establishment. The moment he received the order, he approached Maya requesting that as the officer he cannot be the assisting the chief as the secretary. She had no choice but place her witty assistant as secretary. He was simple honest and witty person, young person who was only educated person in his family and reached to this stage of life by working on his own, good in statistical information, technology friendly and was willing worker. The new witty secretary started working, She started teaching him English, manners of a secretary this was additional responsibility she took on her so that chief does not face any problem.

It was second week of July; the students were to be admitted to the new programme through entrance examination. Her assistants dealing with website helped in developing the module so that online registration could be taken place, the leader helped them for designing the same. She became very friendly, Maya team decided to give full support and she seems to be genuine.

The entrance examination was conducted on a Sunday that was 15th July and the leader invited few subject experts who helped them to correct the papers and after which interviews were conducted, the whole process was completed within 8 hours. The Leader thanked Maya. Very next day Maya received a bouquet and sweets from Leader with a thankyou note. In return she replied her was our duty as the establishment.

It was last week of July, the chief was in little furious mood, his attendant informed about his mood when Maya just reached the office as she and the finance officer use to travel together and that day the finance officer became late by few minutes and due to which they reached late. The chief was in his office doing his work. Maya reached with her usual cheerful mood. Though thinking why he is in ferrous mood. He started his rapid fire round, without even giving her chance to speak, when he finished the firing, Maya very politely in same tone reminded him that he has given the task to some other officer and not her. He said bring the duties of each officer and keep a copy with him. Maya again informed him that said copy is already in his right drawer of the table. He looked at her and said then why you did tell me before. The officer was called and had discussion regarding the task given by the chief by then she had left his office as she was too busy with the preparation of starting a new institute. Again in the afternoon she received call from witty assistant, **"Come down Baba has called upon you", I asked him what could be the matter, he said "*do not know, mood is not good, atmosphere is tensed.*"** Maya rushed down to his office, again rapid fire round and did not allowed her to speak. He wanted to know whether the work of new institute is completed or what is the progress. She informed him the progress and also brought to his notice that it is the responsibility of establishment when new institute is to be established and placed before him the relevant rules. He read the rules and was satisfied. But Maya didnot understand why he was so furious. But he admitted that she has lot of patience which is most important when you work in an organization because you have to handle people with different nature, temper, psychology. **This was his sixteenth teaching/commandment**.

Just one day prior to the inauguration the of new institute, things were not in order, Maya took her entire team with the permission of chief and with help of academicians arranged everything and changed the entire look, the champion was little happy with her because Maya extended full cooperation. The entire office all worked late night and next morning again with the team was present at 7a.m. Maya requested the chief to inspect before the inauguration, but he was very cool and said he will come at the time inauguration directly.

All the authorities and dignitaries were very happy and appreciated the work. The Management was very pleased with the initiatives taken by chief. The function was over, the chief was to give lecture and after which we have scheduled another leadership meeting. Maya rushed to see the meeting arrangement and just wanted to go through the agenda and notes so that could conduct the meeting smoothly. The chief's sent her a message to attend the lecture, but she was to attend the next scheduled meeting. Maya was told by royal man that his lecture was excellent. The chief was in good mood, he after finishing his lecture, came to his office and informed that today the proposed new officer identified will come now to meet him. Maya was happy because she knew the person. The person arrived and was taken to chief's office for a meeting. After the meeting the chief called her and informed that the person identified is not willing to come for administrative post as he is academician and would like to contribute his experience as academician. He would read her mind and console her that soon he will identify someone. They attended the leadership team meeting and there the chief appealed the leadership team to give priority to research and publication, the establishment academic quality is known by its research work.

Maya received sms from her witty assistant, "chief has started his lecture". She replied him "when did stop giving lecture". The chief was totally engrossed talking about research work. Finally during the meeting, she reminded him by sending a small note that we are running short of time as other agenda item are pending. From that day onwards, the chief started becoming little friendly with them.

During the second week of August, It was Thursday, she was travelling in the bus and the Finance Officer was next to her as their vehicle was sent for servicing. She received call from the vice-commander, first question was where are you? She replied in the bus. She said please donot jump with the joy, as she had some good news. Maya said is it we got permission for our new centre. She said no no it is relate to you. For a second she thought may be an extra increment in the salary. The news of her promotion as the officer was communicated to her, but she was strictly told not to express and further the chief will communicate to her the good news. Maya was on top of the world. She wanted to reach as early as possible to the office and meet the chief. The journey of 30 minutes to the office was of 3 hours.

After reaching office, as usual she went to chief's office, the witty assistant was with chief taking his directives, she waited outside his office. The witty assistant came out and said *"from today onwards whenever you will come to the chief office you donot have wait outs his office, you can just walk in, these are directives of the chief" chapter close* Maya just smiled at him, as was getting impatient to meet the chief.

But soon her dream were scattered, after greeting him, the chief started giving her directives regarding website, why the publications are not mentioned on the website, why staff details are not yet uploaded on website. Maya thought how ruthless is the chief, knowing the news still not even informing her. She decided that to will obey the orders of vice-commander and wait and see till what date chief does not inform her.

Maya requested his secretary to call for the officer incharge for website, the chief said no need to call the officer, it is your responsibility to get it done. Further he said start preparing the compliance, which is required be submitted to authority. Actually chief was testing whether she is following his teaching or not. She smiled and left his office.

After some time, again her witty assistant informed her: Mujrim Hazir ho. chief has called upon you. She went down, there was a big problem related to examination and revaluation. He said sit down; the officer incharge and other subordinate officer were already in his office. The chief was in serious mood, the officer incharge explained the entire matter, it was requested that a small sub-committee to look into the matter and recommendation be placed before the chief. Soon committee's recommendations were placed before the chief, but there was blunder on behalf of the officer, before the decision of chief he has already accepted the recommendations, the chief was little serious about the working of the Officer. The chief has his own style of transferring non-performer from the establishment; he called Maya and informed the HR dept. to transfer the officer incharge to some other small institute.

Maya was taken aback, this was second case of transfer, but the chief was very particular he had habit for procedure always consult the vice-commander before taking any decision or implementation of any decision. Maya asked him are you taking decision in hurry? He replied, I never take decision in hurry, I always observe, study, give enough of chances to a person and even after all this, again there is non-compliance then I take decision, which is good for establishment otherwise the establishment cannot grow because of this kind of non-performer, which are hurdles, this is serious mistake and may bring the reputation of the establishment to an stake. **This was his seventeenth teaching/commandment.**

That evening during their laughing session, her witty assistant said *"Baba has fired one employee, others be careful"*. Everybody became serious, and looked at Maya; the non-performer cannot exist in the establishment that is the message from Baba.

Two days were over, the chief did not informed me about the promotion, Maya thought probably he is still in thinking stage or not sure about his decision.

On the occasion of independence day, that was his first celebration or he was to hoist the National flag, the chief reached before time, the function went off well, the chief spoke very well, the message was for the young generation, their behavior, their contribution to the society by large and their duties towards their parents and Nation. As the establishment, children from orphanage were taken care by providing those, clothes, study material, some good movies, some cultural events classes, etc. Children from the orphanage were invited to perform, which frankly Maya did not appreciate, why they should be called to perform in front of us, Maya was thinking that these children might be feeling that just because the establishment provides them necessity as a compellation they have to perform and the establishment would feel proud of themselves that they do charity. But did not get chance to express her views. A photo was to be clicked with the chief and those underprivileged children. The chief was ready for the photo and suddenly she heard him calling Maya for the photo.

It was sure that, chief is able to read her mind as what is going on. After the photo he said this how the world showcase their charity and become popular, so as the management, they have to exist in the world as page three personalities.

The cultural event was well organized by another leader; the chief appreciated the entire event and declared that he would have lunch in coming week with the participants who have performed so well.

After the breakfast, *her witty assistant said" I hope chief remember to give lunch " till date the these participants did not get opportunity to have lunch with chief.*

It was 16th, suddenly Maya received call from the management office to come with some important documents and simultaneously the secretary to chief called Maya that chief has asked her to reach within 30 minutes to the management Office.

Maya immediately left, when she reached there the HR told her that she have to appear for an interview, immediately and he took her to the committee, Maya was literally pushed in. As soon as enter, she saw chief as the chairman of the committee and was little nervous as was not prepared for the interview and other committee members were from management council and outside expert. The question answer session began, she was giving all the answer, the chief asked her if you are given a chance/opportunity to become statutory officer, you will be called as what? She was not getting the word which was well defined. He gave her clues and she immediately answered his question. The interview was over, after coming out, *her witty assistant and his secretary said" Congratulations and celebrations " but donot forget your tiny assistant" She said nothing has been so far declare so donot announce on radio.*

After some time Maya was called by the vice-commander office, where both the childhood friends were having gala time. After some time, she was called inside, the vice-commander congratulated her and said that we have decided to give you promotion as the statutory officer of the establishment. She turned to chief and asked him whether she will be able to handle the post or perform her duties, he nodded his head and said hmm, as he was busy reading sms in his mobile. After finishing the reading he said YES. Maya thanked both of them and came out. *Her witty assistant said" now you are satisfied, when I was informing you, you did not believe. She* returned to office, first she met **her** friend Finance Officer and informed her about her promotion, the joy and appreciation she had for Maya as friend cannot be described.

It was 17th and was full moon day, the chief during the morning briefing session asked her did you receive the order, Maya said no but wish to receive today being an auspicious day. He immediately called HR and instructed to issue the order, the chief left for some meeting with the management and in the evening there was a book release function at the office of the management and it was mandatory for them to attend.

The chief called her at about 3 p.m. and enquired whether she has received the order or not, at 4 p.m. the secretary called and said you before coming for book release function meet HR. Maya knew the order is ready. First she met the vice-commander with whom was closely working for last 5 years, after thanking, Maya was directed to collect the order from HR who was waiting for her. Maya accepted the order, first thing she wanted to see her salary, which was most important component after thanking HR, immediately rushed to the function, where the chief and the vice-commander and royal man were on dais. The chief looked at her with a question mark on his face. She text him and the vice-commander thanking them as she received the order. The chief read the message and there was smile on his face.

Next morning, Maya handed over the order to chief as she wanted to receive the same from him. He congratulated her and said please read your responsibilities as prescribed by the authority and no deviation from them. You have been given more responsibilities then before. He asked the other officer togather the entire staff as he wishes to address them.

The witty assistant was waiting with his comments said" Baba (chief) has loaded madam with lots of responsibilities, Baba is testing" but he till now doesnot know her capacity of working, soon chief will realized. She just smiled at him and told him "you will meet me in the evening during laughing session at that time will discuss"

The chief addressed the staff and communicated them that Maya would be second officer in command.

After the address, the chief told her why he did not informed her four days earlier, because he wanted to complete the procedure of selection as per rules so that nobody should point out that as favour has been done to her. She was recommended by royal man. Never deviate from the procedure and norms. The management on their own should appreciate your work and feel that you are fit for the post. Maya knew that he was waiting for her to break the news, but again the procedure and norms are to be followed. **This was his eighteenth teaching/commandment.**

Slowly they were getting use to the chief, his publications and research work became centre of attraction, almost every day his articles were published. He made people aware what research means and how to publish papers nobody was till then even paid attention to it. He taught the staff how to publish the papers, they were to learn how to put the data of publications, which the authority wanted them to project, she did not know how to do. He called her and taught her and her team as how to compile the research publications and project to the authority and at the same time to be uploaded on the website,

During the month of August, the chief was very busy streamlining the research activities of the establishment, he instructed her to discuss the research scholars' admission with each dean and place all the details before him. She followed his directives; one by one each discipline admissions as the research scholars details were placed before him, more than 50% admission were not approved by the chief. The effected scholars started visiting the establishment, they started approaching the authorities but the chief was very firm about his decision. He directed his secretary to direct all such effect scholars to her. The disappointed /angry scholars in groups started approaching her, after giving patience listening to them made them aware of the rules and regulations and handled them with lot of care. Some of them approached the management where in chief deputed her to be with the vice-commander. The vice-commander supported the chief and agreed with his decision. She followed his eighteen commandments. The matter was resolved the Management appreciated chief. But chief's research did not stop here, he wanted to know who has instigated scholars and with his own sources found the person who was instigating and was spoiling the brand name of the establishment, immediately transfer order were issued as per his 17th commandment.

The message was very clear to one and all that under no circumstance dishonesty, spoiling the reputation of the establishment would be excused,

The chief by this time became very popular among the leadership team, scholars and staff.

The chief started visiting other institutes under his control and started addressing the students, giving them the opportunities to enhance their talent and start involvement in research. He firmly believed that is need of good mentors/educators, who can impart knowledge, the young minds can do wonders and it is their first duty to return back to their establishment and Nation. The knowledge enhances if it is shared, imparted. He wanted to motivate the young minds and wanted them to be involved and take the establishment to greater heights. **This was his nineteenth teaching commandment.**

The chief for a long time was feeling that establishments under his control were working in isolations and there was need for consolidation and revisit the programmes offered by them. The Management was very happy with his idea and started giving the chief full support. Soon a committee with the external experts was appointed. The chief himself invited them to help the establishment to consolidate the establishments, so that weakness could be addressed. There was great movement of the era. The leadership team was not very much in favour because their freedom would have been controlled and they were to follow the system.

But since the chief convinced the management and also the members of reputed of management council. The committee started their work in full swing.

Her witty assistant said: Baba (chief) has marched to bring revolution and corrective measures but how far he would successful, let's see how many walk with him and makes him successful or he walks alone. The establishment was taking serious turn in a positive direction this change was for good. The leadership team gave full support to the committee and the report was discussed with the Management and with chief after deliberations with royal man. Probably chief knew that what he is doing will benefit the establishment. The report was further discussed with the management council, the report was studied by eminent personalities/academicians were happy with the same and approved the same as it would be part of progressive establishment. But some of the members from leadership team and also so called advisors were not being academicians, could not think of /apply /understand the impact/ Laurence which the establishment will earn out the whole exercise. They started adversely brief the royal man and vice-commander. The royal man was in dual state of mind, and was not able to decide or provide directions. He finally very wisely requested the chief to place the report before the managing council and on the other hand he requested the members of management council to forward the report to him, so that he will study the same as he wanted to gain some time. The members followed his directives. Till date it is mystery. It was a unanimous decision of all the members of the leadership team to invite the chairman of the committee to the establishment, so he could be of great help to implement and take it further the process of consolidation.

This was a threat/challenge to the management and also some of the leaders, because the power would have been divided and the leaders would have forced to follow the system/details which required to be delivered to the learners in true sense.

The egoism of some selfish small mind people was more predominant than the progress of the establishment and they did not want to give credit to the chief for the movement in education of the establishment as they were the "royal man" of the establishment. But chief being scientist, a simple person with high moral values did not understand the thought behind. The royal man was feeling that he would be losing his "Satta" "territory" since he was very well known in the education sector.

The chief took it as one of his failure as if many failures were in his cap.

The chief wanted to enhance the quality of the leadership team as well as the knowledge providers, he started head hunting and whenever he could see the talent he brought them to serve the establishment, eminent personalities started pouring in due to chief's reputation, as if the entire sector were with him and ready to help the chief. He became more famous then the "royal man". He recruited over 100 scholars to be wings of the establishment, who would help the establishment to fly to greater heights.

Her witty assistant during our laughing session said: Kite is flying in the greater height and chief has really controlled and his grip is very strong, now nobody can stop the progress of establishment. The chief was becoming unmanageable as if his feet were on accelerator, he being genius believed in innovation, soon a young innovator as recommended by one of the prominent genius was invited, the so called family members of establishment were amazed with the progress going on in few months after the arrival of new chief. The young innovator was first introduced to the vice-commander and HR, they had couple of meetings with him nearly it took few weeks to reach to the establishment (Maya was wondering he in innovator, if he is taking so much time to reach the establishment then what he will do as innovation, how wrong I was at that stage (which she never understood in the beginning) how much time he would take. The innovator arrived with big bang; the moment he arrived he submitted a big list of his requirement to her. Maya asked her colleague, if he requires this entire requirement than what he will do. Her colleague said all these are in budgets have been sanction, you donot interfere. The innovation cell was established. The young innovators started working contacting the leadership team members explaining them the concept and what they would do, but again the leadership team lobby was so strong and they would resist and not allowing any new concept to enter. The chief during the meeting with the leadership team introduced the innovator and everybody started slowly responding to him. The chief was happy that young minds are working together. The young innovator once visited the mess and was shocked when he saw the amount of food being wasted by the learners. He decided to bring some innovation so that learner realized the value of food, which they get from hard earned money of their parents. The innovator discussed the issue with the chief. The chief called upon her for discussion and also wanted to verify what the innovator is saying. The task of reducing the food wastage was taken by the innovator, the chief connected her with him so that the innovator has full details with him and also support.

The innovator was brilliant person, he involved the learners in this exercise and announced/stipulated the condition that who so ever participate in the exercise would earn some credits, the learners were excited, but these days learners are not focused they are "ratoo totas", they believe in getting marks and a job, whether they survive in job or not that is there secondary thought.

The innovator with a small group of 30 learners made a beautiful, meaningful document, which was simple but carried right message for the learners. The document was discussed with Maya and some other officers, after viewing the document, Maya could not control her emotions and her conclusion was anybody seeing the document would never ever waste a single grain of food.

The chief was informed about the document and was request to be present during the presentation of the documents before the learners. But as usual the chief was busy with some other innovative ideas ---.

First time witty assistant was quite, she concluded that this is the right way to communicate to the learners and also it teaches them the moral values in life. The innovation team presented the document before the learners in small groups, the demands from the groups increased and the innovator has to repeat the document several times. But this bought a change in minds of young learners, the wastage of food reduced to one fourth. The document finally as decided to upload on the website so that more people across the global will be benefited. The chief was happy also they did knew that he was well aware of happenings at the establishment. He appreciated the young innovator; he said as per culture, the food is treated as God and wasting food in other words insulting Food God. You have taught the learners the true meaning of respecting food god and made them aware of culture and tradition. **This was his twentieth teaching or commandment,**

Her witty assistant said: Baba (chief) believes that any change is always good.

The innovation cell did not stop here, they wanted the learners to decide as to what they you prefer to learn, the permission of the chief was another issue, because he was very busy with research, patent, whole day typing writing for newspapers, getting angry on staff if they commit some mistake, we as the staff were use to his behavior as he was scientist and we were firm believer that there is a very thin line between scientist and a psychic person.

The young innovator approached the chief and sought his permission for such competition, the innovator's office and her team extended full support and finally the competition was announced, the special designed reproduction were send to all the establishments/organization, uploaded on the website, nearly 20 teams participated, the curriculum so submitted by the learners were sent to the external experts, the assessment report was not that great, only one team won consolation prize.

The young innovator was little disappointed with the participation of the learners. The report was placed before the chief, he smiled and said Good. The young innovator was forced to think what is good about it. He asked the chief what is good about it, he said first time in the history of establishment, the learners were given opportunity to express what they would like to learn, further it is an eye opener that the quality of education which we provide is not upto the mark and probably not at par with the industry requirement and society by in large. The mentors and the knowledge provider have to increase their quality of teaching, at present their knowledge seems to be very hallowed. One should always remember what ever work we do, should have full knowledge of the subject and then only young minds can be turned to good citizen, academician, and expert in their filed. One has to be dedicated to the work. **This was his twenty-first teaching/commandment.** The Young

Innovator was encouraged and once again was ready to start another new innovation for learners.

Her research on the chief was becoming very complicated and was beyond her capacity to understand him. **Her witty assistant said: Donot waste your time, baba is special brand blessed by God.**

While innovation was the talk of the time, one learner, who was not educated in term of notchess but probably was truly educated, he was trying to make a windmill which is a machine that converts the energy of wind into rotational energy by means of vanes, with limited amount of energy. The young innovator could not effort his research as his resources were very limited. The chief wanted to give him an opportunity and provided fellowship for six months. But as usual, in the research field probably people are more jealous in nature and always does not appreciate any other junior person to progress, until and unless the senior is also involved and given preference. The poor innovator was innocent and was only involved in innovation. But the Head of the institute was miser person, who use to believe in himself and did not wanted to give opportunity to young generation. After working for six months, the head submitted an unsatisfactory report. The project of the young innovator was closed and for whatever he has spent time and his talent, as promised a fellowship was not paid to him till the end. He made a request to chief, the chief as per protocol reminded the miser head, but he gave deaf ear to chief's request. After the innovator left the fellowship, the miser head made as the project for his own student and started working on it, might be successful as half of the research has been completed and the remaining credit will be taken by miser head and will please the royal man.

Her witty assistant said: Baba trust everybody he doesnot understand the world is full of crooks .

The chief was concentrating on the academics; he wanted to improve the quality of academics. To assist him a dean academics was appointed. But soon the chief realized that he was not much of help. To support the chief in typing, give him secretarial support one executive was appointed. The chief called Maya and requested her to train the new secretary, as she was not from the same field and did not have experience of education establishment. Slowly the smart secretary started picking up the work. The chief was also little relaxed because he could get some secretarial assistance.

The first commandment of the chief was communicated to the secretary; as usual without thinking the new employee always say yes to everything. It was soon revealed that the secretary was another tiny tot. The secretary was reporting to the vice-commander the movements of chief and also whatever was happening at his office. All of them became very cautious and careful because we're not sure about the quality of reporting. The Management funda was to get the information and not the quality, whether the reporting was genuine, factual, to the point. They were interested only getting the gossip.

Her witty assistant said: From frying pan to fire......

The chief decided to offer research programme to the postgraduate learners so that after their post-graduation they get opportunity to peruse their research and in turn, the establishment will get research scholars and knowledge providers for future/ educator. Maya decided to support and assist the chief as she could feel that dean academics was not that active as required for the progress of the establishment. The chief took the task on himself and applications from learners duly approved by the educators were invited. The vice-commander has one learner who was reporting the progress on the proposal, the new initiatives taken by chief. The chief instructed her to send the applications to experts for evaluation with time bound evaluation report.

The evaluation reports were placed before the chief, but he had something in his mind he wanted selection process to be very vigorous and hard-hitting. A few external experts were invited to interact with the applicants where the chief was one of the members. After interaction with the experts the applicants were required to write about their research topic and send to the her and as per the directives and process, the another set of educators were appointed to evaluate the same. The chief was to leave for the his second trip to USA, the some of the evaluators submitted their evaluation reports, but some of them did not follow the deadline. The office was to submit the evaluators report to chief before he was to leave. The establishment was following with the evaluators and Maya was getting worried as the selection list was to be established next day and evaluation reports were yet to be received. By then the chief left for the airport, as per practice she text him whether all arrangement are in place?

He replied yes, but what happened to the evaluation reports from educators. Maya informed him that some are yet to come and selection list is to be establish next day. He could feel that she was really very tensed and helpless. He said not to worry, he asked Maya to send all the papers submitted by the learners, he evaluated all the papers at the airport as he had 3 hours for evaluation of 15 papers, she obeyed his order and after 3 hours just before boarding the chief sent evaluation report with his approval. Maya had no words to express; she spoke to him immediately and thanked him for extending full cooperation and help. He said: A true leader always come to rescue of his team members and not let them down in any condition. She knew tomorrow the list of selected candidates is required to be published and you are alone to face the situation, he will not let you down. **This was his twenty second teaching/ commandment**.

Next morning during **her** briefing session with **her** team she shared the incidence and also the thought behind the same.

Her witty assistant said: The chief works more than anybody else and he too workaholic.

It was October, the second quarter report was due, Maya kept the draft report ready which was due on 10th, but the chief was away, she send him the draft report, but did not receive any reply. After chief returned from his foreign trip, he was once again reminded of the report and the date report was over, he provided his inputs but appreciated the draft report submitted, Maya was worried what would be the reaction of authorities the report is delayed by 10 days. She was neither finding suitable words to express apology for the delay nor there was response from chief. As worried officer requested him to provide the final approved copy of the report so that with the covering letter it could be sent to all. As usual his x"ray eyes could understand her concern regarding delay, he said here it is, donot worry I have resolved your worry. Just below the title of the report, chief mentioned extended report, her worry vanished and there was smile on her face he too smiled and said by now I know you, your are efficient worker. Maya came out of his office and **her *witty assistant said; Baba (chief) has resolved your doubts and if you any more he might resolved them also.***

That evening at 7p.m., she received the call from chief, appreciating her efforts and efficiency. Maya was wondering what wrong with the scientist, but did have time to think as compliance reports were on priority.

The vice-commander asked her about the progress on compliance required to be submitted to authority, she said it will ready very soon and will be submitted to the vice-commander and her.

The chief arrived on the stipulated date, Maya had quite a few piled up papers to discuss with him. The moment she enter his office, he said where is the draft compliance report ready, she was carrying the same. He had cursory glance and spoke to the vice-commander. First time he made her felt that academicians are much better than the administrators. He invited one of the educators and requested to prepare the report and informed that she will be assisting the educator. She was really very upset, inspite of working on the report 24X7, which was written in official language, why the chief was not happy. In her 28 years of dedicate service this was the first time her report was not accepted by chief. He could read her mind and said let educator feels that their involvement. Maya and the vice-commander were not comfortable with the chief decision and so as the educator. The educator had never prepared the report nor did she have full background of the situation. But finally the vice-commander said let them try. She informed them there is not much time left for trial and error method. The chief got angry and said, I am responsible and not you for the report.

Maya shared her concern with the team, we all came to a conclusion that let them realize the work they have completed and when the report would not be in the correct form again we should not entertain again the request.

Maya started assisting the educator. This was first time in such depth the report was getting ready, this was the most important report, She was thinking and did not wanted to leave any chance so that history of 2000 does not repeat. But new chief was abdominal. The educator started amending the draft report submitted by her, because it was exactly as per norms its contents were full data and progress of the establishment. The educator completed the first draft report within 8 days, the draft was sent to three of us, she pointed out that report cannot be written in future tensed, when there are only 9 chapters on which we are required to provide details, it would be advisable not to add the two more chapters. But the chief was very adamant, but the vice-commander agreed to her first suggestion and educator changed the tense. The vice-commander informed her that this first draft will relook at it after changes are made. The educator /academician sent the second draft, it was festival holidays and on the day of festival she was assisting the educator till 2 p.m. in the afternoon. Did not enjoy her festival holidays. But at the same time was very angry with the chief. The chief instructed the educator to share the report with all the leadership team so that everybody is well aware what is being sent to authority and if some points are missed that can be incorporated in the report. It will be a team effort. His firmly believed that academicians can only perform better. A few members of leadership team provided their insight but which was not of much use. Maya was still upset with the attitude of the chief. The chief believed in participatory governance system. **This was his 23rd teaching/commandment.**

Her witty assistant said: Why you take it your heart, Baba (chief) doesnot know what mistakes he is making.

Her inner conscious was still not agreed with the report, but had no choice or voice her opinion, though in the establishment has a precedent that each one can voice their opinion atleast.

A meeting with the royal man, chief and the vice-commander, educator and few more members from leadership team were invited to discuss the report. The royal man gave few inputs and soon after she wanted to place her inputs, the chief said: Since the report is approved by the royal man subject to inputs provided by him lets us finalize and submit the Authority, he appreciated the efforts put in by the educator.

Her anger was on 'satve asmanper', She just walked out, but the vice-commander understood that there are still some corrections and which she is trying to bring it to the notice. But did not wanted to cross the decision of chief (Childhood friends) supporting each other. But an external expert had the same opinion as of mine.

The vice-commander came to her office and said will incorporate the suggestions, which you feel is right and genuine, Maya provided the inputs and were incorporated, but was still not satisfied because of two new chapters added in the report.

Her team members requested her not give any suggestion, they will learn their lesson from their mistakes.

Her witty assistant said: Madam, you know there are three kind of people in the world, one who learns from others mistake, other learn from fall into problem and learn and third one who learn from their own mistake.

The chief approved the report and sent to Maya for finalizing administratively and directed her to submit to the authority next day. Probably he did not want her to read the report and give **her** unwanted uncalled opinion.

Before the report was sent for final prints, Maya called chief and requested him to look at the publication annexure and sent a through one of her assistant instead of she taking it to him.

He felt why Maya did not take the details to him, his ego prevailed him from going through the annexure, he in stern voice directed his new secretary to summon her. Maya reached to his office, the chief in angry mood said; have you forgotten the protocol, she did not reply because it was her mistake, she would place the papers before him, Maya submitted her apology and requested him for his directives. Since she accepted her mistake the chief smiled forcible and agreed with her that some stylistic changes are required and he returned with the correct way of presenting the same. After making the stylistic corrections, his approval was obtained. By then the vice-commander also provided inputs and finally after getting approval from all the report was printed at the printer because it was magnanimous task, which within few hours was not possible with the infrastructure facilities at her end. She was to submit the report next morning. At the same time two more compliance reports with reference to deficiencies pointed out by another two statutory bodies were also to be submitted and the royal man instructed her to make it to the point and after making the same it was approved by all authorities including the chief.

The reports were ready at about 2 a.m. and Maya was to leave to submit the same to authority by 6 a.m., She left at 6a.m. and text the chief that she is on her way to submit the report. He did not respond to her text thinking it was not necessary as the cold war between she and chief was on regarding who is more efficient academician or administrator and Maya was not convenience with the chief and still not convenience.

After submission of the reports she called chief but he did not respond, the vice-commander immediate responded was happy the reports are being submitted. Maya scanned the copies of acknowledgments received from all three statutory bodies and submitted to chief, the vice-commander and royal man. She spoke to one of her fellow colleague from the authority and both of us went to have lunch as the colleague was accompanying her since morning and she wanted to enjoy lunch as last three days she hardly ate anything. After having lunch Maya took leave of her fellow colleague and went to market to get some sweets for her team, which was her normal practice and always wanted to thank her team for their hard work. Maya purchased some sweets and left for the airport.

Next morning, the sweets were kept on chief table before his arrival and it was reminder to him that he has yet to give us his joining sweets and also festival sweets, but probably we were wrong, these thoughts were never occur to him.

Her anger was still on higher side, which chief did not bother.

There was very important event /ceremony scheduled, she was secretary of the sub-committee, the chairman was efficient, meticulous person and was from the management and a close relative of royal man, he was adopted child. Though he was scholarly person but in his really life he could not take decision without the permission of his wife. The famously known as Yes man to his wife in short term everybody use to call him JR.KG. The chief guest of the event was first eminent personality. The preparations were in full swing, duties and responsibilities were allotted to some of the members of leadership team. Everybody was on toes, as there were many security procedure the establishment was to follow. The chairman of the committee as per protocol was reporting to the chief and vice-commander every day. Again the office timing were extended by an hour, her team was really tired of working without break for past so many months. As per directive of the management two eminent personalities were to be honoured by honary notches at the same time scroll of honour were to be prepared for both of them. The chairman of the committee sought chief advice for writing /preparing the same. The firm believer in academicians, the chief asked him to allot the job to educator. The chairman communicated the chief decision to Maya as the secretary. The details of both the eminent personalities were provided to educator. She knew the educator well and was not sure about efficiency since writing scroll needs specialization in writing, which she had her own doubts, but was to obey the orders.

The chief had a very important conference to attend where he was presenting a paper. Every day chief was following the orders issued by her regarding extended timing? His secretariat was busy with his speech and also his paper which was to be presented in the conference. Maya was managing, coordinating, like a anker with the protocol officers of the state and central as the First Citizen was the chief guest for the function. Just before a week, Maya received call from the chairman of the committee, he was in furious mood, said that: writing the scroll is the responsibility of the Officer of the establishment and quoted the byelaw, which were brought to his notice by royal man.

She very politely replied him, Sir: this is what I was trying to tell you but unfortunately you all are firm believer that the academician with good english would do best job and hence the responsibility was entrusted on a English educator and I have communication which you have signed so as chief.

He replied agreed with you, but the draft prepared by educator is far below the standard and we are in crisis state and now as per rules you are responsible to prepare within 24 hours.

Maya immediately called the vice-commander for help, she said, the chairman of the sub-committee has requested me to stay out of the issue and expressed her inability to help.

The only her saver was chief, she called him he was in conference, did not reply her call, she text him urgently required your help. The chief was very kind enough to come of the conference and called, her anger bust on him, she narrated the whole incidence to him. He was cool as ever. He said: we cannot do much at this stage, but he will speak to the chairman of the committee, mean while he gave her to references to which she could approach for the help. The chief did not know that last two occasion, she was writing the scroll and was appreciated by the royal man. Again after few minutes he called her and said that he has spoken to the chairman of the sub-committee and as per rules Maya was supposed to complete the job, she would have brought the rule to his notice.

Maya replied him, now there is no time discussing the issue, now we have to complete the job, will do it. On your return will discuss.

Maya contacted both the references; they too did not have experience of writing scroll.

Her Witty assistant said: Madam, when you know that you have to do the work and time is very short, nobody is coming to your rescue. How true he was at that moment.

Finally, at about 8p.m. on **her** way she took all the relevant papers at home. After reaching home started writing till 3a.m. and knocked the door the of her old experienced educator and a mentor to Maya, he was waiting for her as on previous evening she had already briefed him.

He welcomed her and said when you will stop working 24X 7, don't you feel tired, she said: I have removed word tired from her dictionary. He said thats why I call you guru. He served me hot coffee, he said enjoy coffee and I will have a look at your draft. He went through the draft scroll and made some minor corrections and pat her back and said do your people value your work or you are as usual not bother. She said Sir you know me, no body bother about me. He laughed and she left his place.

After reaching office, she emailed the draft to the chairman of the committee and also the chief. Both of them were astonished that how come Maya finished **her** work. To get the approval of chief was most thorny job. The chief immediately responded with few modifications/corrections. The draft was sent to the vice-commander and also the chairman of the committee. Both of them approved and appreciated the timely help extended by her.

Her witty assistant said: **A good boss makes his men realize they have more ability than they think they have so that they consistently do better work than they thought they could"**

The chief reached back from the conference and very few days were left for ceremony. She waiting for his arrival and during the morning session, she put all the evidences regarding scroll and brought his notice that details were seen by him and the Chairman. He agreed.

The chief was busy writing his report, first time the annual report was ready in time, the copy was placed before the chief, he glanced it and said good job.

Just one day before the ceremony, the protocol officers were on their high pitch, the Chairman of the committee did not turned on sight. In the morning the royal man as usual arrived that day, the ceremony largest flag of the establishment was to be hoist, she and chief left for the ceremony and after the ceremony the royal man confirmed that all arrangements. The protocol officer met the royal man and pointed out that there is spell correction required to be done in Hindi at the entrance of the campus. The royal man immediately called her and asked her being local language speaking, why it did not occur her, Maya firmly replied that this was already pointed out one year back but the project department is in process of correcting it. The royal man got little irritated and ordered Maya to get it ratified by next morning. One more last minute responsibility on her shoulder, soon the royal man left the premises.

The Management Council members were reached the establishment and were in guest house.

Maya was totally busy with the arrangements and add-on responsibilities. The vendor was summoned by her and requested him to make necessary corrections as the royal man has given permission to go ahead with all the arrangements and was not required to take any permission.

Maya got message through a messenger that such a grand ceremony is the responsibility of the chief and the chairman has played his role well and vice-commander also made a excuse of falling sick and did not turned up to the venue. The chief looked worried, but did not wanted her to know the facts it was the question of childhood friendship.

There was huge discussion between her and the protocol officers and the security. She was running out of her energy, the chief did not leave the office till 8p.m., the eminent personalities were in the guest house, a dinner was organized and the chairman, the vice-commander did not attend. Maya reached to chief in his office after completing the all the protocols and security issues, he felt that he should be provided with a glass of juice. Just to divert her mind from the huge responsibility, he said just listen to my speech and let me know whether I have not missed any important points and also keep a check on time.

He started reading the speech and while enjoying the juice she was listen to him after he read, there was silence in the room. He was waiting for her inputs. After thinking for few seconds she said" it is giving the feeling that some dog is chasing you and you are reading very fast now". He laughed and said what to do you have given me few minutes to speak; he said he will reduce the length of speech in the night. He was getting late for the dinner with the dignitaries who were waiting for him. After completing the work and also the correction in spell, her team left office at 11p.m., Maya called chief and informed that all arrangement are being taken care off, he said all of you come for dinner, but we were already late and next day was early reporting.

The next day was the ceremony a grand ceremony, the chairman of the committee arrived early as last night she expressed that he would have been on the premises with me. But she was use to his style of last minute putting the responsibility on her shoulders.

The chief arrived at the stipulated time, she was on her way to the venue, he saw her walking toward the venue, he stopped his car and both of us reached the venue, after inspecting the same they came back to his office, again he said now listen to my speech. He read the speech which was ok but not very impressive as she thought it to be. But did not discourage him as there was hardly anytime left for the function.

The chief guest was to arrive after an hour, suddenly the chief and the chairman asked to her to get the permission from the protocol officer to add one more chair on dais. Maya was about to get heart attack. Chief smiled and said do it.

Maya instead of asking permission, informed the officer as to what change we are doing on dais, he happened to be her old friend, he said "You will bring me introuble" she did not even bother to listen to his approval and acted upon the order of the chief.

The programme was flawless, perfect in all fronts, everybody congratulated the chief but Maya could feel that vice-commander was little reserve with the chief.

After the grand success of the programme immediately there was lecture by an eminent personality who had come from foreign county, the vice-commander and royal man did not attend the lecture, the chief took over the responsibility of being there and contribute during the lecture. She was feeling something fishy but did not dare to ask the chief. She was asked to attend the lecture and it was very inspiring and it left deep impression on her. Maya was fully charged to contribute to take the establishment to greater level. This lecture was arranged because the chief has taken a lead to prepare vision 20/20 document, he wanted eminent personalities to share their experiences with us so that we get inspired and started working towards the betterment.

After a few days, the all entrance examination was scheduled and was conducted without any hiccups. After the examination next day the establishment started getting complaints from the applicants state that there were errors in the question paper, it was alarming, She immediately forward the communication to the incharge of the examination. As the day progressed the complaints started pouring in, the social networking sights were also talking about the same errors. It became non-manageable. Maya contacted the vice-commander and the chief, the vice-commander said it is responsibility of the chief. The chief said we will look into the matter. Next morning the newspapers were talking about the same.

Maya called chief he said reach to office as early as possible and also request the incharge and dean academics to come for an emergent meeting. Soon after her conversation with the chief the vice-commander called who was in furious mood; because as per procedure the only spoke person to the media was the vice-commander, how come the dean academics gave the statement with whose permission. Maya was not aware of the development, she mentioned that according to royal man, she should be aware of such a important issue since she was the official spoke person.

The emergent meeting was held and it was decided that with the said issue to be investigated and report to be submitted to the chief. The dean academics was given the responsibility to submit the report after detailed deliberations with the examiners/paper setters etc. The dean academics became active and called for the details and had meeting. At about 5 pm the chief called Maya and asked whether the dean academic has prepared the report, by then the dean has left the office, he was worried that the establishment prestige is on stake and being responsible for the examination, how could he take it very causally. But ultimately he was friend so could not do much.

Her witty assistant said: You will be targeted every time, people are friends and in friendship adjustments are bound to happen.

The next morning the chief called for the report, it was revealed that there were five errors in the question paper and the dean academic was responsible. As all the question papers were approved checked by the respective chief educators. The chief looked very tensed and worried, he requested for external expert opinion. The experts opined the same that there were five errors in the question papers. The chief instructed Maya to let him know the past history.

Maya placed the records before him and also informed him the facts that every years (atleast last three years) there has been this kind of errors in the papers and the establishment is being giving benefits to the applicants.

He lost his cool and spoke to the vice-commander they had discussion on the same, the vice-commander reached the establishment and asked Maya to produce the documents after seeing the previous documents was feeling sorry for the state of affairs. The chief took a stand that as per the documents the management is responsible for the entrance as it was approved by the management, inspite of bringing the rules and regulations to the notice of management. But when there are crisis, people always raise their hands.

The chief was still not tired for inventing/introducing best practices, new initiatives, inspite of experiencing no support from the management, he probably wanted to do his duty and thought the dirty politics behind his back.

It was February month; the chief was still not clear about certain processes and the role of the management and the establishment. He could feel even day to day routine work is also being reported to the management and without having complete picture the decisions are being communicated. He wanted to place all such issues before the management council, he was the man of principle and never wanted to deviate or have irregularities which would come in the progress of the establishment. The finance officer was not able to perform her duties well despite of having many years' experience with her highest professional notches to her credit. There were many such matters which the establishment was responsible and was to be discussed with the members of the management council.

He directed Maya to include all such issues in the agenda; the agenda was discussed with the vice-commander, before it was issued. The vice-commander agreed that roles and duties are to be clarified.

One the day of the meeting, the vice-commander and other internal members were present before time, the chief could guess that this is unusual and he informed that please bring all the relevant papers, rules and regulations in the meeting. As per the establishment rules the admissions to any programme was the responsibility of the establishment. But the vice-commander though during the preliminary discussion agreed to empower the establishment in its sprit and letters, but during the meeting the internal members and the vice-commander did not agree with the proposal which was placed before for consideration. The chief placed before them the rules and also informed that when there are crisis and some mistakes take place, the management raises their hand and the establishment officers are answerable to public. The vice-commander did not appreciated the item for discussion and also requested that same practice be continued and a big amount of revenue and surplus was at the credit of the management from the entrance examination and actually the management did not wanted to empower the chief, they wanted only the rubber stamp. The agenda item was for deferred and was decided to take in the next meeting. There were items regarding the financial matters and the clarity on the governance system. Because as the chief of the establishment had not authority to take the decision. The leadership team like a autonomous establishment were reporting to the vice-commander and decision were taken without the knowledge of the chief.

Though on many occasion it was mentioned that the chief would take decisions related to academics, research, administration on behalf of the establishment and he would consult the management if it required. But there was so much resistant from the vice-commander and as per rules any decision where the majority of the members give their consent, it would be treated as the final decision. The chief and three external members could not succeed in implementing the rules as the governance system did not exist.

Finally the management council requested that the governance system manual to be prepared on priority with a period of one month.

Her witty assistant said: *one month means how many working days?*

He started talking about the road ahead and what should be the vision of an establishment. He started discussing with some of eminent personalities, academicians, experienced persons in the field. One by one they were invited to the establishment to guide the leadership team, staff and others. This was another massive exercise the chief has initiated. After few session, he realized that the officer at the establishment has been entrusted with many responsibilities and as per his firm believe in academicians, requested a committee of academicians to process, complete the task and put-up to him.

As usual as per the psychology of people, if the leader doesnot take lead in completing the task, it becomes no man's land. Again after few weeks, the chief inquired about the progress. Finally an external expert, well-wisher of the establishment was requested to help the committee.

He was very sincere, dedicated, truly learned personality, started visiting the institutes, discussion, meetings with the various stake holders. The exercise was conducted for more than three months. The draft was prepared and was sent to chief for his approval, but the chief had typical psychology, when he used to give cursory glance and if the document is not up to the marks, he used to withdraw himself from the project/proposal after giving his true opinion.

The chief has nearly completed one year, he was feeling contented that the brief vision and plan for the next five years, as communicated to the leadership team and colleagues at the establishment from the very first day, is progressively taking a request from of an academic driven and research oriented establishment.

He appreciated the expert who had made great progress towards achieving its objective. As a part of the collaborative process, interaction meetings with the leaderships team, the future plans as an integrated though would further developed to support a comprehensive document.

How positive was chief, may be because he was simple, scientist, who believed only working and did not know the politics. The moment the draft reached to the vice-commander, the thought was why not to take credit for the full exercise and prove existence in the academic world inspite of coming from medico-political world.

The vice-commander took the responsibility of completing the document spending hours together to discuss, editing, giving creative, insights and directly connected with the royal man. Finally the document was ready for release. The committee was well appreciated in public and so as the vice-commander. There was a mischievous smile on chiefs face, which was unpredictable. When the document was sent to the establishment for the record and also for uploading on the website, as procedure whatever is to be for the public, the officer of the establishment always read. It was another disaster, the proof reading, the compilation of the document was far below the standard. It was brought to the notice of the chief, he said; the vice-commander has compiled, and it has to be correct and he will not interfere. Maya requested the vice-commander and also the members of the committee to relook at the document as it contains errors. The vice-commander did not agree at the first instance, but after going through the document, the vice-commander agreed. But the documents was the responsibility of the vice-commander and the blame could not be taken. Vice-commander has never experienced failure in life and never wanted to accept the truth. The whole blame was put on the external expert.

Maya was summoned to the vice-commander office and was asked for the explanation regarding the payment made to the external expert, inspite of many error in the document. Very politely she replied you have approved the document and also the payment as she was requesting you to go through the final contents of the document, but you all gave deaf ear to her suggestion.

The final blame was on the chief, since he invited the external expert and did not perform his duty as the chief of the establishment.

Maya knew that the Management has started their old game of cornering the chief and starting with their tactics of keeping the chief under their thumb.

Maya spoke the truth to the chief and promised him that she will support him, he was little happy but he knew how to face the crisis and control the situation. He said the officer in second in command is responsible for the official correspondence and will upload the apology publicly and also give the benefit to the applicants.

Her witty assistant said: baba (chief) taken the right decision and for once he stood by your side..

That day on her return journey to home Maya did not stop to take peanuts, which every day on her return use to stop to buy some peanuts and who so ever use to with me use to share. The driver stopped at the groundnut wala and purchase the same and offered to her. He said Madam, why you are so upset; slowly you will know the true colors of the people.

Next day it was Sunday, whole night Maya was thinking why people play dirty politics and for what, why the dean academics did this? But could not get any answer.

On Sunday morning she sent chief the thought for the day which was:

"A bird asked a bee, u work so hard to get honey & people steal, don't you feel sad?

Bee sad- no because they can never steal her art of making honey.

Soon after that Maya received letter from chief, directing to send to all the members of management.

Maya immediately obeyed his directives, soon the response for the external members of management council, stating that for routine procedures the members of management council are not to be invited. But the members from the management were very happy to receive the communication and some of them visited the institutes to oversee the procedure. The vice-commander was very happy with the move.

Her next task was to complete the draft rules and regulations which were almost ready; Maya had many sessions with the legal advisor of the establishment. After detailed deliberations with the advisor, the draft was placed before the chief but he was very busy.

She was really following with him to look at the draft, on the day of annual cultural event, she requested him to spare some time and look at it. He finally agreed to have look at it, both of them started comparing the draft, soon the vice-commander arrived and was little disappointed so see that instead of enjoying the cultural event were busy with the official work. She commented:

You are very good in following up and does not allow anyone to rest in peace till you complete the work.

They realized that, the vice-commander was not very happy to see that they as team are working. They could sense her intention and soon they joined the cultural event. The staff has really worked hard and participated in the cultural event and won the prize, this was the year when the establishment had won many prizes.

After few days, the royal man asked the chief to submit the new rules and regulations draft so that it could be finalized and submitted to the authority. The chief asked her to forward the draft to royal man and vice-commander. It was a daylong meeting, where legal advisor was also present and after detailed discussion, the document was finalized.

Soon it was decided to submit the document with updated compliance report to the authority; as usual she was on toes. After completion of the document of rules of the establishment, the chief as a procedure got the approval from the management council. It was very happy occasion that the establishment has accepted the new rules and regulations.

The updated compliance report with the new rules and regulations were submitted to the authority.

The establishment was marching with the flag of the progress.

The authority after reviewing the document decided to meet the chief with officers of the establishment in the month of March. The establishment received the communication in the last week of February, the chief decided to give gist of report to the committee in order to give over all view of the establishment and progress.

The chief shared the gist report with the leadership team and also prepared the presentation so that time is saved, the chief with Maya, other leadership team members and the vice-commander were invited to meet the committee so that the committee could offer their comments on the compliance report. The committee met all of them and discussed the progress of the establishment.

The chief did not want to put his best foot forward. The members were known to the chief and they were well versed with his style and knew that he will present the factual picture of the establishment.

This was pre-review meeting and the committee opined that the compliance report was voluminous and the information is much more than required. It would have been as per the parameter provided. The vice-commander just looked at Maya because she and another external expert have submitted our opinion which the committee is just informed them. But chief was firm and wanted to put his views before them. Finally the committee gave patience hearing and chief gave the complete picture of the establishment. The committee informed that they would again meet the in the next month. They directed members and chief to prepare and submit synopsis of the compliance report giving only the comparison of three years in a tabular form and not exceeding 20 pages and only one parameters stipulated in their communication.

The team returned back and started working on the same. The same educator was requested to make the report, the educator prepared the report, submitted to the chief, the chief after giving glance, lost his cool and asked the educator to be more careful in making the report and requested Maya to assist the educator. Finally Maya and educator spent lot of time and prepared the report and submitted to the chief, he was still not happy with the report and their thinking of reducing further without changing the contents has stopped, Maya and educator admitted their limitations.

The chief called Maya, she accepted that whatever they have prepared was final from our side. The chief looked at her with anger and said hmmm.

Maya left his office, by the time Maya could reach her office, the chief has corrected the report and a crisp reported with the stipulated number of pages was ready and he sent the same on her email.

She was really surprised with his speed of working, the moment she received the mail, Maya rushed to his office, and said: Sir, when you have already corrected the report and final version than why you were angry.

He said this is the difference when an academician applies his mind and prepares the report. She had no words to express. The chief has already hit her tight on her face, and left her with no argument which was incomplete regarding academician verses administrator. The chief was happy with his very miniature victory.

Her witty assistant said: You were told that chief (Baba) will make it unnecessary you tried to solve the pazzal.

The chief had completed his one year and he wrote to the royal man stating that he has been given 6 comments, 9 suggestions and 3 guiding principles remains her inspirational guiding force. And he has given best to bring revolutionary changes in the establishment academics and administration and he strongly feel that we are moving in the right direction towards our goal to make establishment truly world class establishment. While he thoroughly enjoyed one year association with the establishment, have experienced and encountered with few challenges. His priority was to transit the establishment to a world class establishment. Therefore, his main focus during this year remained on this challenge and most of his actions were aligned for progress towards this objective.

As everybody knew, we were in advanced stage of review from Authority and are moving ahead in the right direction. His presentation before them was appreciated and the committee appeared positive. The authority by than was asking us specific and 'evidence based' compliance. It means for every claim we were to must provide supporting documents which were mostly related to academics and governance. Further he mentioned that there are many overlapping areas especially of governance between the management and the establishment. There are no clear governance manuals. As per the Authority new regulations the establishment is required to function independently with the chief as CEO. In practice this is not happening and it is very important to bring clarity on his expected role.

He further expressed that presently he is not playing much decisive role in HR & Admin (appointments /assessment/ review / promotions / transfers / termination, legal matters, campuses), Finance (purchase / investments / budget allocations/ re-appropriations), Infrastructure (campuses, hostels, mess, sports, recreation, maintenance, expansion / new campuses), Academics (number and admissions of students, process of admissions, student discipline, student extension and social services, extension, expansion and new programs, international affairs). All the leadership team members were supposed to functionally report to him except sending their leave applications as a formality. He wanted royal man to think wearing a cap of chief when he is expected to function as CEO, but in reality, no academic leadership reported to him and he has no financial, developmental or HR powers. It is like expecting optimal performance from an executive with tied hands and legs, plugs in ears and blinds on eyes. Actually he was managing the functions: With help of Management of the establishment he managed routine administration through statutory officer and senior officer, regulatory compliances, research & innovation, faculty prospecting and development, special initiative like Vision 'revisiting programmes offered' – Innovation Cell, new academic and research collaborations, industry – academia collaborations, PhD program, developing research projects, guiding students, editing Journals, writing research and popular articles, working in authority committees, giving talks in conferences and provide leadership and general advocacy in education. The chief was legally responsible for several functions especially related to administration, HR, and Finance but has no actual authority. The decision making process is not professional based on frame work of establishment rules but is more spontaneous and *ad hoc*. As the three was overlapping of roles of chief and the vice-commander.

In such a situation where there are dual or shadow authorities, the staff was bound to get confused, stressed and underproductive. This has also a danger of thriving inefficient sycophants over honest professionals. Recent *de facto* termination of one of the important officer and attempts to harass and threaten officer were few recognizable fall outs. The chief was concerned about the environment in the establishment which was not healthy and conducive for bringing excellence to move in the direction of world class. He expressed that unless these issues are addressed its root cause, the establishment administration will only deteriorate. The establishment needs to be managed professionally with help of competent people and statutory bodies. We have given undertaking to the authority formally accepting the new regulations of the authority and it was the duty to follow them. He sought the guidance from royal man regarding management and the establishment to have mutual and complementary roles in respective governance and the new regulations in letters and spirit to govern the establishment?

The chief further expressed that he would like to discuss these issues with royal man and vice-commander at the earliest convenience. He was discussing the issues with his childhood friend and also sharing his concerns. How wrong was chief thinking that vice-commander would have kept royal man informed. As he would like to have an open ended meeting preferably after office because they could spend some quality time to discuss and arrive to some workable solutions to improve establishment's governance system.

His communication was real bombshell to the Management. There was lot of turmoil at the management level. The chief became a threat for them, because he was a person with principle, integrity, brave, which was not accepted by the royal man. In the present circumstances the royal man doesnot need a brave, honest principle person, but needs "Yes Man"

Her witty assistant said: They will take him to the task and he will walk away, there are many people with him but you be very careful you are alone and you need job.

Soon the royal man and the vice-commander had a meeting with the chief and discussed how to bring the establishment to transit from better to best category in the review process by the authority The consensus were that the management office and the establishment office were like two wheels and they must take proper care to keep them aligned, supportive and complementary. The developing a clear governance manual is very important task which was to be completed. Some of the provisions from new authority regulations were acceptable to royal man. These mostly concern the authority, eligibility and other issues regarding royal man, appointment of chief, issues related to property. The chief did not had any issues on these matters. His main issue/concern was about professional management of the establishment as per the authority rules and regulations. The operative part of new regulations, which dealt with establishment governance through statutory bodies should be strictly followed so that the establishment is governed independently.

It was agreed that chief should be able to function as CEO with help of statutory bodies.

He firmly believed that any dual authority structure will not be conducive for healthy ecosystem of the establishment. The dignity and authorize of the post of the chief should be maintained and he should be empowered by ensuring that the key leadership team works directly under him.

He further wrote his few suggestions, which would help the chief to govern the establishment professionally in the true spirit of authority expectations:

All policy matters related to new institutes, facilities, campuses, financial relations, should be done jointly by the management and the establishment.

All matters related to legal proceedings, court matters, land dealings, acquisitions etc should be done by the management in consultation with the establishment.

A small group may be appointed to develop a authority manual especially where there are gray or overlapping areas or lack of clarity about the functions between the management and the establishment.

All academic and research functions should be governed by the chief as per the rules of the establishment.

All administrative and HR functions should be managed by as per the rules of the establishment. All leadership appointments, performance appraisals and revisions should be made by the chief in consultation with the vice-commander.

All the statutory officers of the universities should be empowered to perform their duties and should be made accountable for their respective functions

All purchases should be done by the establishment as per the rules in consultation with the management

The routine administration should be left to the chief and other officers. As far as possible any direct interventions by any one should be avoided.

It is also important to keep establishment authorities especially the management council fully informed. As professional and participatory practices should tremendously help to create healthy ecosystem and efficient establishment governance.

The royal man and the vice-commander did not take the suggestions of the chief in the true spirit and one fine day, Maya received a call from the vice-commander stating that the management has decided to file the case against the authority rules and regulations and asked her get the same approved by the chief and leave immediately for filing the case from the Hon'ble Court. This was the reaction to the chief's concerns.

Maya rushed to the chief and communicated the directives received from the vice-commander.

The chief smiled and said he is aware and he further instructed her to prepare a detailed note for the members of the management council members as he believes participatory governance system and would not like to deviate for the rules and regulations.

The chief informed the royal man about his decision of getting the consent from the management council as the management council is finally responsible for the all the legal standing of the establishment.

As per directives of the chief and the vice-commander, a detailed note was circulated through email to all the members of the management members, the establishment received positive response from the internal members who were from leadership team. But no response from the external experts on the management. It became matter of concern for the chief and royal man, the establishment was not able to communicate its decision to the vice-commander. The atmosphere at the establishment was becoming little tense and tricky. There was pressure from the vice-commander for Maya to leave immediately and sign the papers on behalf of the establishment. But as Maya was reporting to chief and the decision of management council was awaited, could not do much.

The chief sought guidance from one of the most reputed, experienced member of the management council and he guided correctly that since the establishment is already submitted the compliance and also given an undertaking to authority, it will affect the evaluation of the establishment and its reputation and also it would badly reflect on the members of management council.

The Management started harassing Maya because she was the only person who was authorized to sign the document (official) on behalf of the establishment.

Two days were over; the establishment was yet to receive the consent/descent from the members of Management Council.

First time that evening, Maya received threatening call from the vice-commander; She finally decided to disturb the chief at the chief's residence and narrated the episode.

He permitted her to leave next morning but wait for the decision of management council and uphold, till further orders.

Next morning she left, the moment Maya landed on the airport, the protocol officer was waiting for her, she was surprised to see him and was not expecting such a VIP treatment. The vehicle was waiting for her to take to hotel where other officers from the Management were already waiting for her arrival. The moment Maya reached she received the call from vice-commander asking her welfare. After reaching hotel, Maya contacted the officers and all of us met and discuss the issue. The legal Advisor, mentioned that till he doesnot get communication from the vice-commander and royal man, will have to wait and after the approval the petition would be filed. The whole day there was no communication inspite of the three met for breakfast, lunch and evening tea. Maya had a word with the chief, he informed that he along with one of most senior eminent personality who in past hold very senior position in authority, well read, learned personality, was advisor to authority on many committee, met and tried to convince the royal man. The other eminent personalities on board of management, who were well know persons, scientists, academicians, person of repute, also tried to convince the royal man and vice-commander, but it seems the royal man has already taken decision and still we would wait for a day, probably he would think about the existence of the establishment first and would always wish to bring the establishment in highest grade.

Maya thought how wrong the chief is? He still doesnot know the true nature of royal man, once he decide will not rethink. Whether the establishment's image is damaged or not. She was like a prisoner, in a house arrest. The whole day nothing happened, no communication from any authorities.

Maya was very positive that second day everything will be finalized, but her thinking was not correct, till evening no communication from any authorities.

Third day, took the appointment of the senior prosecutor, who was well versed with the rules and was encouraging to file the petition, thought that he is doing his duty as prosecutor.

The chief has again provided the management a nuclear bomb stating that the establishment does not come into picture at all in this matter. As he not see any sound academic reasons or valid grounds for the establishment to join the to file a writ petition challenging legality, validity and applicability of the new regulations in the High Court. The management council which is the principal organ of the management and the principal executive body of the establishment has formally accepted the new regulations and accordingly have adopted rules and regulations which is now effective and binding on the establishment. A strict compliance is very important to enable establishment's transition to highest Category. As the authority is actively going through various parameters in relation to compliance In the capacity as chief, he has submitted in writing as well as have stated during the presentation before the authority that our establishment is sincerely and honestly complying with the provisions of new regulations as prescribed by the authority under the respective provisions and notified in the authority of's official gazette. The final review and decision of authority was still awaited, which would have direct implications on the very existence of establishment. Moreover, this issue is also being heard before the Hon Supreme Court of, where the establishment has given undertaking that it shall remove all the deficiencies which have been pointed out by the various authorities within the time granted by the three authorities. The decision in this regard is still awaited. Although, our establishment has not received any documents to study relevance and applicability of these cases before taking such an important decision. Therefore, he can not deviate on any ground from the commitment, which I have made as a chief on behalf of the establishment to the authority. The outside experts on the Management Council have also categorically expressed their dissenting votes / views with necessary justification, which is quite in tune with the above points. Therefore, in his capacity as the chief of the establishment he is duty bound to protect and safeguard the interests of the establishment and its all stakeholders to make it truly a world class establishment.

The establishment rules clearly, states that 'it shall be the duty of the chief to ensure that regulations and rules of the establishment are duly observed and implemented; and, he/she shall have all the necessary powers therefore, under the provisions of establishment rules again requested to intervene in the best interest of the establishment.

Further he expressed his regret and inability to implement the decision passed by its managing committee in the meeting directing the establishment to join the write petition challenging the legality, validity and applicability of the new authority regulations He was very optimist about such an action will help us to maintain high stature of our establishment and also not jeopardize our efforts to bring the establishment to category of highest rank, which was first priority mandate.

At about 11am, received a communication from the chief stating that as per rules, the majority of the members have accepted that the decision of the management but the external /experience/academician/members submitted their dissent. The chief as the chairman had to accept the decision since the majority of members expressed that the establishment has to file petition against the new rules and regulations. Maya informed the members who were with her. It was evening she thought of offering her prayers to god to give wisdom to everybody. she left the hotel room, the representative searched her room which was against the ethics or moral. The hotel staff informed her that due to some emergency expressed by the colleagues, they have provided the keys of her room. Maya was really helpless, decided that will not interact with them and only sign the documents as per rules.

There is a proverb in English which says that pen is more powerful than sword.

It was Sunday, Maya informed her officer to book her return tickets as she did not want to wait anymore. He said he needs directives from the chief, Maya tried calling chief, but failed to reach him. she decided to book herself and informed the legal advisor, who had very good knowledge and expert in law, he was alumni of the establishment and was most faithful to the royal man, HR chief and of course the vice-commander. Basically he was knowledge person but as a advocate even if the client admit sin, but he would try and safeguard the client and twist the case in the client favour. He respected Maya, because last so many years on many legal fronts, and cases Maya supported him and the establishment and they together got many laurals in legal matters to the establishment. Maya informed him that she needs to return back. He immediately got into action and prepared the necessary documents and obtained her signature. This time protocol officer was not available at the airport to say saionara.

The chief was waiting for her arrival, they decided that after bringing the establishment in highest grade they will quit the job.

Her witty assistant was missing her for last four days he said: Please be careful of tiny tots, minute to minute information is telecasted.

The establishment filed the petition against the authority policy and got the status quo order.

The Management was very happy with the development, but it not in favour of establishment. The Authority review committee was shocked because the chief was well known for his honesty, is vision, wisdom, he has never deviated for the rules and regulations, where ever he has worked, it was always in the best interest of the establishment. The establishment progress was on priority than the personal issues. **This was his 25th teaching/commandment.**

The news spread across the education establishments and also among the academic world that because of egoism of some the reputation of the establishment was at stake.

On her return, Maya was informed that the royal man and the vice-commander had a confidential meeting with the leadership team and willfully kept the chief away from the meeting. In meeting the members were briefed about the loyalty toward the Management and the royal man. The loyalty of the establishment officers were at the wager.

It was unbearable situation, tiny tots were on their prime misreporting mission.

The chief was in helpless condition, because of his descent, the management was not good mood with the chief. Slowly the rift between the management and the chief started expanding. The communication between the chief and the royal man was almost stopped, it was a great insult to the chief inspite of knowing that he has to represent the establishment before the authority, they rub the wrong shoulder. The chief decided to write few lines again to clarify his stand he mentioned his great concern in the interest of the establishment reflecting few observations and thoughts in the light of developments. At the outset, he reiterated that his decision not to support the writ petition was only to avoid any harm or delay in efforts to expedite transition of establishment from to highest grade establishment. He had no personal interest or agenda other than protecting interest of the establishment, because the establishment have moved the court and as a consequence the review before the authority might be delayed as it was very important to review present situation.

Ever since a *status quo* was been obtained, the atmosphere in the establishment was only deteriorating. There were all kinds of rumors and false accusations about the chief being confrontational and rebellious against the royal man. All this was happening despite his clear-cut and sincere explanations in writing that he had to take the stand simply to safe guard interests of establishment primarily he was appointed as chief. Actually speaking he was simply doing his duty to protect and preserve the main strategies. However, as he expected, due to the course of action chosen, the authority review process would have indefinitely postponed and its outcome would be determined by eventual decisions of the court cases. He was always thinking that, such a risky option and to his regret none of them did not even consider in depth other courses of action since the decision was taken at the management end despite her well-meaning advice as well as sincere persuasion by outside experts and few others.

He wanted the royal man to know that it was wrong precedent to call for the meeting of the leadership team of the establishment in presence of selected members of the establishment and management mainly for ensuring their personal loyalty. It is very hurtful and unfair to point fingers at the chief without shred of evidence doubting his deep rooted loyalty to the cause of the establishment, despite his unshaken and ever assured respect for royal man and unstinted cooperation offered to vice-commander in all fronts. He felt that he was deliberately excluded from such an important meeting which only added insult to injury.

In such a situation it is very important to get clarity on royal man's views as to where does the chief stand and if the royal man believes that his principled stand was impersonal and was based on the best long term interest of establishment. He was of the opinion that there was a need to develop effective and professional working arrangements perhaps with some lessons learnt out of these developments. The chief again insisted for a good governance manual which might have been a right beginning. On the other hand he expressed that if both royal man and the vice-commander have lost confidence in him or if they were of the opinion that he is not doing right things as the chief, he was ready to step down to prevent any collateral damage.

Her witty assistant said: The war has begun, help Baba (chief) and support him, Madam, you need to take necessary measures.

The management decided to depute one more tiny tot to the establishment under Maya, who was very junior /immature/without any experience, he was relative of human resource chief and most notorious person in the establishment. Maya was informed about his transfer under her by the vice-commander. She had no choice but to accept because he was the relative of one of the officers at the management office. On the same day, she had been to the management office with some official papers and there she saw a meeting with so called relative, was on and Maya was instructed to introduce him to chief immediately. Maya requested for chief's appointment, the chief could visualize the situation and did not give any appointment. Again she was instructed to ensure that the relative meets the chief and start functioning from next day.

Maya met chief on her return and informed him the directives, the chief refused to meet him and the vice-commander did not even thought of informed or discussed the issue with the chief. He directed her to give the appropriate work load. The tiny tot team was very happy as one more new members had joined them.

Her witty assistant said: Madam, please pay attention, you need more soldiers in your army and the number of soldiers has been increasing in the enemy army.

Her good friend the senior officer had applied for leave for two months to go abroad, she was another honest, dedicated staff and which the management did not prefer as she was reporting directly to chief as per the rules, the management decided to terminate her services immediately. But at the same time they wanted the work to be completed by the finance officer.

It was Management meeting and the senior officer had presentation on finance of the establishment, the members including external experts' members appreciated her perceptions on finance matters.

The finance officer and Maya after the meeting walked toward the office and in the corridor they were stopped by HR chief and requested both of us to meeting him for few minutes, they were in happy mood and quickly walked with the HR to **senior officer's office**, after having some chat, he informed her that her services are not required further and he is communicating decision of the management.

It was central shock for Maya and also to the finance officer, they immediately rushed to chief, because the finance officer was directly reporting to him. The Finance officer broke the news to the chief, he too was shocked, being the CEO of the establishment, without his permission the vice-commander and the HR chief has terminated the services of a statutory officer, he immediately called the vice-commander and asked how such an action has been taken without his knowledge. He further said CEO of the establishment he would have been consulted or taken feedback regarding finance officer. The vice-commander said; since the management council of the establishment has delegated the powers regarding any appointment to her, the management has taken such drastic decision. The chief was in real helpless situation, his hands and feet were tied and was asked to walk and show the progress. He immediately sent a communication to the royal man, thinking that he would rethink about the decision of the management, again the chief was wrong and was positive about the people.

Her witty assistant said: They were waiting for her to complete the work and wanted to get rid of her long back. But at the end God is great and he will take care of every one.

That evening, the team members were feeling that the word humanity has been deleted from the world. The finance officer was in mental trauma, next day she handed over the charge and left the organization. The loss was of the establishment as it has lost a willing worker.

During morning briefing, Maya placed before the chief, the requirement for vehicle as the vehicle had cover about an lakh total mileage, the chief recommended the proposal to the vice-commander, meanwhile the officer at purchase department and finance department started completing the formalities, which was required to be completed for purchase of a new vehicle so that the matter could be expedite. The vice-commander has seen the correspondence and accordingly a very meager token advance amount duly approved by the vice-commander was sent to the vendor. All the legal procedure was followed, but did not receive the new vehicle nor we heard the progress on the same. One day it was late in the evening, Maya and her colleagues were travelling back from the office in same vehicle where the dickey was wide opened, one of the colleague was holding the door which never use to be closed, the chief's vehicle just passed by and he noticed that the vehicle is in really bad condition. He immediately called Maya and asked about the new vehicle, she informed him, the same is awaited.

Probably the chief spoke to the vice-commander, next day was another disaster day for Maya, the delegation from the Management including the HR and chief Finance with the vice-commander arrived to the establishment and again there was earth quake, it was firmly objected how can a officer of the establishment recommend that a new vehicle should be purchased and how did the purchase and finance department started the initial procedure, the chief of the establishment had no power even to approve the or recommend the requirement. Maya was lost, did not know how to work, cannot even say anything to chief as the chief and the vice-commander were good friends. But as part of duty, she reported him the incidence. As usual or as part of daily affairs, he wrote a communication to the vice-commander, the vice-commander further lost temper on her, stating that such a issue should not have been reported to the chief.

Her answer was: The chief being the reporting officer, she has to inform the matters related to the establishment. The boss should know everything, was her policy.

The chief ordered her to withdraw the proposal of new vehicle immediately and never ever put such proposal before him, it was a insult to the chief as he has recommended after verifying the condition of the vehicle. Maya withdrew the proposal and communicated the same to the finance and purchased department. The whole matter was wrongly reported to the royal man and finally he had a dialogue with the chief and there were exchange of bitter mails between them.

After a month just before the personal function of the vice-commander the vehicle arrived and instructed that it will be first utilize for the personal function and after which it will be sent to the establishment. Maya took a bitter pill and accepted the same. Maya followed the chief's commandment of having patience.

During the meeting, Maya, as the secretary of the council announced the date of the next meeting. The vice-commander requested to rescheduled the next meeting as there was a wedding during the week of management meeting. The members approved her request. But it was another maha episode which was to be telecasted. The vice-commander and Junior K.G, requested Maya to permit many of the staff members under her control to be deputed to attend the work related to ceremony. Maya was already running short of staff and the final presentation was scheduled to take place in the same month. But she had no say. The preparation were in full swings, almost all the high profile personalities including politicians ministers, eminent personalities were invited for the grand ceremony. Because of the marriage the submission of very important report to the authority was delayed and the vice-commander was not in favour of submitting the same because they had moved to Court and marriage was top priority. The hard earned money of parents and donations were spent to their full extent. But outwardly it was shown that hard earned money of vice-commander was sufficient for the marriage. The highest quality of souvenir were sent to each invitee as gesture, it was a dream marriage. Maya jokingly said to her colleagues: When the entire episode is managed by tiny tot, the episode has to be grand, most popular hit show.

Junior KG, though he was very educated person, but he has no thinking power. Maya had worked with him on various important committees. Though he was very sincere, meticulous in his work, but on many occasions he had let her down and on many occasion he supported. He always tries to do something innovative, but never succeed because he has always have afterthought. But he always likes to be surrounded by his tiny tots. He likes to flirt around. But sometime she felt pity, how can a man be so JKG. May be money makes the mare go. Whatever memberships he is now availing is because of his wife's political connections though he doesnot qualify to be the member on few committee.

One day, the vice-commander called her and warned her to be faithful to the management, Maya replied, am faithful to my work and will think, breath, best for the establishment than the individual.

The chief's movements were under scan, the lower staff were the tiny tot, reporting the minute to minute news to the vice-commander.

But chief did not deviate from his duty towards the establishment.

Soon the authority committee invited the chief to present the progress of the establishment; again all of them started working towards the same. The chief asked Maya to prepare the presentation based on the one which has presented during his meeting with the authority. Her team again started working on the same and the same time the chief has requested the educator to prepare a very brief report giving only the comparison /progress between two periods as stipulated by the Authority. Maya was to assist the educator again.

The presentation was ready and was to share with the leadership team, the royal man, vice-commander and some of the Management Council members. The chief being scientist was in thinking mood while she was presenting the slides and was trying to analyze what would be the best ways or to present the strength of the establishment and that would help to overcome the weakness. But the vice-commander did not have patience, immediately expressed her concern about the chief attitude. The chief told Maya to change the sequence of the presentation, bring the strength of the establishment first. everybody was surprised and appreciated the directives of the chief. The vice-commander was sitting next her, she immediately questioned her about one of the particular statistical information, Maya placed the record before her and also informed her that the report is of specific period. But she wanted to check that whether her team is really involved in making the reports or statistical information. She asked Maya and she gave her the names of her assistants, she immediately called them and asked them, she got the satisfied answer but still she wanted to project that some more information is required to be added in the presentation. It was Saturday, the meeting was concluded at around 7p.m. and she instructed her to keep the office open on Sunday. Maya sought chief's permission, he had no objection since the final meeting with Authority was scheduled on Tuesday and we had only two days in hand to work. Her team worked on Sunday and got approval from all the authorities the documents which were to be presented in next two day.

The members including chief made the presentation before the authority authorities, the authorities were happy with chief's presentation and also he could convince them that the establishment has taken right measure to progress further. The establishment has taken right direction and will be able to show the progress in future, the direction has to be right.

The vice-commander and royal man were really very happy with them and were very positive about the outcome of the meeting.

After the submission of the compliance and subsequently the management was of the opinion that now, the need of the chief was not much; they would always prefer to have their own yes man. The chief was given some hints, the royal man started communication with the chief and wanted the chief give explanation for each and every act and also the routine matter of the establishment. The chief was getting sophicated with the attitude of management. But he did not do anything wrong or deviated from the rules, so he was quiet and performing his duty well.

When the chief had a meeting with the authority official in the month of May admiring his knowledge, his vision, his views on higher education and also the rules and regulations. The chairman of the committee assured that the establishment would be treated in highest category. The joy of all of them were beyond imagination, it was real happy moment and the entire establishment was waiting for the official communication from the Authority.

The Authority decided to invite him as the member of a council, who will recommend the necessary measures required to be taken for streamlining/uniforming the processes. The Authority officials were very happy to recommend the chief; they immediately informed the vice-commander and the royal man. But the Authority was again disappointed as the royal man informed them that instead of chief, it should be royal man or the vice-commander. The authority understood the intention of the management (royal man). But at the same time they also realized the valuable inputs which they would get from the chief.

The authority issued the orders, where in the chief was one of the members. The chief immediately informed the royal man and expressed his happiness because the establishment got the representation in the authority. How positive thinker he was. **This was his twenty sixth commandments**.

Her witty assistant said: This happiness is temporary, royal man will not leave the person if comes in his wicked circle.

How true was **her** assistant, the vice-commander made a representation that royal man should be governing the establishment and not the naukar. The royal man convinced /managed to get the amendment done. The royal man became the member of the council though it took time it came after the departure of the chief.

Her witty assistant said: royal man is royal man the King.

The examination officer was not experience person and was the firm believer of the fact that the job to be from 9 to 5 and nothing beyond that. The chief from date of his joining wanted to have review of entire examination system, he wanted the dean academic and other deans to update him with their reports, but probably everybody was not well informed or read regarding the system. The establishment received a complaint from few students of a particular institute mentioning that there are large number of students have failed by marginal marks. The communication was placed before the chief; he immediately constituted a committee to look into the matter and report. It came to the surprise of the chief that one of the evaluators has deliberately failed a large number of students in that particular subject and that to the final year students. After receiving the report from the committee, the chief decided that all these students to be given a special examination. The students were happy with the timely decision of the chief as it has helped them to pursue their career further.

The chief was in serious thoughts regarding the functioning of the examination department and further the process. His thoughts were disturb, when the revaluation results of a particular institute after receiving the complaint from the student community. He was seriously concern about the same, he requested the dean to form a committee and look into the matter. After detailed investigation it was revealed that the students have managed the evaluators and due to which there was vast difference in two sets of evaluation. The chief was terrible disturb as the brand name of the establishment was on stake under his leadership. He decided to take leave of such evaluator and send the message that such kind of act would not be tolerated anymore and if anyone is found doing the same. The evaluator would lose the job. The academic fraternity was very happy with the decision of the chief. They assured chief that they will support the chief in the academic process of the establishment.

Her witty assistant said: Baba has taken ruler in hand and that's what was need.

The chief, day in and out was only dreaming and working for the progress of the establishment. One day while he was travelling back from the out of station he met one of reputed industrialist and exchanged his views regarding supporting the IT institutes with having collaborations. The reputed personality agreed with the chief and express that he would visit the institutes about who the chief is so positive. The chief did not wanted to leave opportunity for future, he immediately contact the leadership member and it was very late in the evening the reputed personality duly accompanied by the chief visited the institute and the member of leadership committee put his best foot forward and provided detailed academic activity. The leaders from both the institute participate in their collaborative programmes and the establishment received a big fat grant in foreign currency. The management did not like the achievement of the chief and others because the news was flashed in the newspaper where there was no mentioned about the vice-commander.

Soon after this incidence, the vice-commander decided to have learner exchange progamme with the foreign establishment and was successful in signing the exchange offer, soon the news was flashed in the news paper.

The chief after viewing the news, had nothing to say but a smile.

The secretary of the chief was faithfully reporting to the management about the moments of the chief and also some of his research projects. The secretary would also inform about the news items of the chief which would publish so that as a counter publicity the vice-commander would also publish some item. The chief was informed about such secretary missions taking place in the establishment. But as per his principles, he was doing everything in the best interest of the establishment. But any reporting without the permission of the head was against the norms. One day an important detail regarding chief and other staff was to be sent to the extension of the management. The secretary through oversight made error and submitted directly to the HR Head. One of the assistant notice the error and bought to the notice of the secretary, but instead of accepting the mistake, the secretary blamed the staff and was not ready to accept her error. The chief did not appreciated attitude of the secretary and requested the HR head to transfer her.

The message from the chief was very clear, follow the commandments given by him and he would not tolerate any one to deviate from the same whether royal man or naukar.

The chief decided to publish a book to be dedicated to royal man, a naukar thought this would be best gift to him educated royal man but did still realized that royal man is not truly educated. With help of few others, the book which was truly rich in its text and knowledge was ready. A reputed scientists was invited by the chief and all the necessary arrangements were made to release the book. But since the chief has invited the scientist, the vice-commander and the royal man invited two other eminent personality. While the preparation was on for the release, the chief was away for conference and as usual style of his to make last minute changes so that we get heart attack, but we were getting use to his style, just one night prior he instructed that the book to be sent to royal man and the vice-commander, we obey his orders. On the day of release of book, the vice-commander showed unconcern about the chief's presence and was ignoring the chief. It was very prominently noticeable by everybody. I would understand the humiliation he was facing at the time of function but publically nothing could be done.

Her witty colleague said: Till royal man is alive, they will be on the top of the world but after that it is God's will.

Day by day the chief was publishing papers, patents, articles, sharing his insight regarding research, giving "gyna" at various forum. The chief was known for his research work, his administrative ability, the quick decisions were provided by him on any matter. The vice-commander and royal man was feeling insecure and as the same time, were wondering as how the establishment has been progressing in all front since the chief has taken over the charge. The chief has given freedom to his colleagues to do their duties and take necessary decisions and he always supported his colleagues.

The vice-commander was not able to coop-up with the speed in which the chief was progressing. The vice-commander appointed a scholar, who would help vice-commander to publish research papers. Finally after six month's struggle the vice-commander published two papers in an reputed publications. The chief welcomed the vice-commander to the academic world from business world. The vice-commander directed the leadership team to start publishing the papers as it can be published in few weeks, though it took six months to publish two papers. The leadership team was further insisted to motivate other staff to start publishing the papers and each one should publish atleast one paper every month.

Waha what speed the establishment was progress, seeing the healthy competition between the chief and the vice-commander.

Her witty assistant said: madam if we had money we could have published the book. Maya had no answer to his thought because was not an academician, researcher or a writer.

As the chief was performing his duties as per the rules and he slowly started ignoring the vice-commander and all his correspondence were addressed to the royal man and the vice-commander was just informed. The vice-commander was jealous by nature; the dean academics had already resigned and left the establishment. The new academic dean was appointed from among the deans of the establishment. The new academic dean was one of the old employee of the establishment and was phd in playing dirty politics. After the dean academics joined the establishment, only academic activities were handled by dean academics but the vice-commander was least interested in the academics. The vice-commander was more interested in the gossip, where about of the chief. Further the management was also thinking of terminating her service and wanted the dean academics to get all the information/data from me so that establishment is not at lose. A week after dean academics joined, the chief received a communication from the royal man in the evening intimating to him that to discuss an important issue he would like him to meet.

The chief was little apprehensive about sudden meeting called by royal man. The chief asked Maya what could be the matter or issue for the discussion. Maya predicted that it would be the present dean academics may be promoted to the assistant chief. The chief met royal man and returned, he said you were right Maya. The present dean academic has been appointed as the assistant chief, but I am just sending a communication to the vice-commander to check the legality and also whether we can make such appointment in light of present rules.

But how wrong was chief, royal man has already issued orders as per the old rules, they have already lost confidence in chief. By the time a special messenger was sent by royal man with the orders and she was instructed to follow the further procedure. This was another dadagiri from the management and of course royal man.

Her witty assistant said: One more Tiny tot. Cricket team of tots is ready.

All of them were very upset that slowly they were cornering the chief. He was tough person and was ready to face with his small strong tiny tots.

The management had decided to introduced ERP system two years before, but the progress was very slow, the establishment has extended full cooperation and instructed all the other establishments under its control get into the learning process so that it will be very easy for all to have processes well define and will save lot of time it will be perfect in terms of data, the history etc.

Since the chief had joined, he was asking for the report, first few months I was able to give him the report, but slowly Maya was side track from the committee and could not brief the chief. In every leadership committee meeting, the said issue was discussed and not progress was noted. The chief finally decided to form a committee of academician (his favourite people as full faith in academicians) but the committee also could not do much and was not very confident that the vendor so selected for implementation would be able to complete the work.

The chief called for the report from the Finance Officer, she was newly appointed in place of then finance officer, though she was qualified, but had hallow knowledge of education system and the chairman of the subcommittee, who was well qualified person, he too did not had any experience in the educational establishment.

Both of them submitted the factual report. The chief had detailed discussion with both of them.

The chief called Maya and instructed her to prepare a detailed factual note giving details for last two years. Maya prepared the same and submitted the same to him, he was happy with her factual report. The chief was worried about the payment made from the establishment accounts, which was huge and the outcome was not satisfactory.

The chief had a dialogue with the vice-commander and also with the royal man about the ERP and they too were worried about the same. The chief had further communication with the royal man and briefed him about the amount spent on the project without placing before the management council. That alarmed the royal man and he started looking into the matter. The chief wanted to have external committee views on the project, he wrote his opinion to the royal man. The vice-commander was upset because, the finance was looked after vice-commander. They communicate to chief not have external expert opinion, first to have an internal meeting with the officers and the committee appointed for the ERP implementation.

The chief called for an emergent meeting of the officers and members of the committee. The committee members were little worried, tensed, because the chief would ask them any questions. The chief instructed Maya to prepare the agenda with detailed notes on each agenda point.

The agenda was ready late in the even prior to one day of the meeting and since it was an emergent meeting as per rules the agenda could be circulated just before the meeting also. The chief approved the agenda and gave necessary inputs at 12midnight. The members saw the agenda early morning and were in the miserable state. The next day an emergent meeting was scheduled. All the members of the committee were called by the vice-commander of study the agenda and to be prepared the detailed process on ERP so that they would be place before the chief for consideration. The meeting started at the stipulated time, the members arrived just before the meeting and were in furious mood because the agenda was too detailed and length.

In the meeting, the chief wanted to see the evidences especially for the payment made and returns was not very encouraging. There was not satisfactory justification provided by the committee, the chief was totally pushed to the corner by the members, the vice-commander insulted chief in the meeting, which were against the ethics of any meeting to affront the chairman of the committee. The vice-commander was trying to protect the members and also that whatever happened in ERP was as per the rules. The meeting concluded with a bitter note and the chief could not bear anymore insult from his subordinate and left the meeting.

Her witty assistant said: Truth always prevails.

Maya have never seen chief in the anger mood before; he called for the finance officer and instructed to put-up the detailed regarding functioning regarding financial powers vested with the management and the establishment, which was pending with finance officer for quite some time.

The chief left for the day, after an hour or so she received a call from chief; and he took out all his anger of the world on Maya. She had nothing to say but tears roll down her eyes. First time in her life she felt, somebody without her mistake has exterminated, without her fault.

Her witty assistant said: People take out their anger on their own person.

Doctor said: How could you bear all this alone Maya? And wanted to know whether any skeletons left in the cupboard?

Actually, all this happenings were because the chief was a professional, honest and did not expect that the establishment will be run as the business where nobody could voice their opinion. All ten years of existence of the establishment there was nobody who would think about the progress of the establishment and quality too. That's why the establishment was not placed in highest category.

The office was close for the day, next morning, suddenly there was a call from the chief asking her whether she is aware that new network administrator has been transfer to the establishment.

She replied No, her reply he found very dry. He said what is the matter, Maya did not reply anything. She had taken leave due to her personal commitments. Again there was a call from chief after 15 minutes asking, whether her email is working. She checked and replied no, probably there is some network problem.

He again lost his cool, he said all the internet facilities have been taken control by the Management and none of us are able to access our mails. He said when he entered the office a new network administrator was in the control room and when he enquired with whose permission he has entered the security room and has taken the control of the establishment.

He immediately wrote a communication to the royal man about the incidence and also communicated about the conductive atmosphere of the establishment. She was told there was literally quarrel between him and vice-commander. He never wanted me to leave the job. Though to all the new appointees he warns that I am very strict person and doesnot spare any one. But she donot believe any one means any one.

Maya was so busy with the personal commitments, was not able to reach to the establishment. The land line phones were taped and also the phones were under scanner.

After an hour, Maya received called from the vice-commander asking to send the minutes of the meeting, which was held yesterday and instructed to send immediately within an hour.

She immediately drafted the minutes of the meeting and sent to all the members, who attended the meeting. The internet facility was provided to only for an hour till she has sent the draft minutes to the members. The moment the mail was sent, again the mail was closed. She informed the chief about the same. He too was not able to understand the mafia way of approach of the Management.

The chief called for assistant chief and discussed the matter, the assistant chief express concerned and the mafia way of capturing the establishment process and creating deteriorating atmosphere in the establishment.

The day progressed, the chief decided to have a legal opinion regarding EPR issue specially payment and also the outcome not provided by the vendor. He send a communication to the Legal Advisor of the establishment.

The chief thought that the legal advisor may give the true and correct opinion. How wrong he was; the legal advisor was faithfully to Management and not the establishment. He immediately informed the vice-commander. There was lot of restlessness in the establishment.

Her witty assistant called her and said: You please come to office Baba (chief) is in frustrated mood and probably disaster will take place.

But unfortunately, she was so occupied with her own commitments, could not even thought of attending the office.

The chief called her in the evening and asked whether the establishment grading has come as he was informed about the other establishment grading. After finding the same, the authority informed her that since our case is in the high court, the grading will be communicated through the court. Maya informed the chief accordingly.

It was evening, she missed the call from chief, after some time again called him, and that was most historic moment of her life, the chief said" Maya I resigned......

She said what and why how could you do this? He said I was trapped and had no choice but to resign.

She asked him what is the matter: He said, the royal man is stating that he have written a letter to authority committee against the establishment. But I have not written any letter to any one expect whatever was officially communication about which you are well aware.

Maya immediately called her fellow colleagues at the authority and found out the truth, it was other way round, the royal man has written letters to the authority committee about the chief and not the chief.

She was pained, worried, annoyed, disguised and what not.

The soon after the communication with the chief, his secretary called and informed about the resignation of the chief and his office has to be cleared and his belongings are to be sent to him.

The chief directed all of us not have communication with him; otherwise we all would be in trouble.

All these historic events were taking place on Friday, the vice-commander, instructed the campus administrator not to permit Maya and the chief to come to office till next working day. It was another shock, could not understand the logic behind all directives.

There were many rumors regarding sudden decision taken by the chief but many friends, well-wishers especially from academic circles many of them we're expressing concerns and inquiring about the reasons behind the chief's resignation. Frankly, it was not an abrupt decision. It was in making for last few months during which major issues cropped up, which were related to governance of the university vis a vis role of the management in the establishment management. While there were several valid reasons, series of incidences, which ultimately resulted in the resignation of chief. The well-wishers wanted chief to share his reflections on the situation especially because they have direct implications for the growth and development of higher education in our country. Finally the chief agreed to give his personal reflections.

There was great demand from the well-wishers to publish his reflections and also upload on the establishment's website, but Maya being second officer in command could not fulfill the demand of the well-wishers, because the family did not gave her permission to do so.

Maya was nervous, anxious, did not knew as how to make his reflections to reach to people, she was trying to meet the demand.

But she and her team decided to follow and will keep following his commandments throughout our life, which really helps mental peace and job satisfaction.

On the next working day the acting chief that is vice-commander reached office before the scheduled time and occupied the chief's Chair of the establishment. And the humiliation started from that day.......

The establishment received a communication from the authority asking for the explanation for the illegal appointment ie not as per the new rules.

The vice-commander (now the acting chief) thought that she had communicated to the authority, but she very politely said, the website speaks itself and further placed before her the evidence that the assistant chief has directed to put her profile and new designation on the website.

Doctor said what happened than-- she said of her officers informed her that probably the management wanted her also to resign with the chief, but some wise person advised them that two top positions cannot be vacant at the same time. The thought over and decided to be give me some grace period.

The security around me with number of tiny tots were also increased.

On the same day, suddenly at 5 p.m. a communication was received withdrawing vehicle facility from me. By then the buses left the campus, I was left out, that time I felt very sad, humiliated and insulted. But all these feeling were of no use, because I was expecting humanity from inhuman people.

She called for a private vehicle and travelled back home. Next day onwards travelled by her own vehicle.

Her witty assistant said: All wicked people/officers will now through their tantrums, to the highest degree of harassment will be in your lap.

After the chief's resignation, the life became miserable at work place Maya was the target for humiliation, all the matters which were in process, establishment's reputation, research activities, routine administrative work and what not. But it was very unfortunate that not a single person in the world could understand her feelings. Her hard-work, her dedicated service, honesty, sincerity, loyalty was not even thought once before humiliating her. Maya was totally isolated from everyone, it was like "chakravyuha" but courage and commitment were so strong, that she never cared. And stood alone and without a bow, with of sight several tiny tots shooting at her. In a way, it was harassment, mental torched in the battlefield of education sector. It was the biggest breach of ethics and code. This was the turning point of her career from the establishment.

According to the chief the academician are very learnt persons, intelligent, good human beings. How wrong was his perceptions, these so called academician were the only one who were involved in creating a circle or boundary, setting limits for Maya.

The vice-commander held a meeting with the leadership team where she was also present, a well-cooked story was narrated by the vice-commander, Maya was instructed not to note the same. The leaders were coward; they did not have courage to correct the vice-commander but believed each and every word.

The vice-commander was advice by some experienced person as that soon a very important ceremony was scheduled and it was the prestige of the establishment and the work was to be completed, the Chairman of the committee requested her to concentrate on the work of upcoming ceremony. Since working hard is being in her blood, forgot that she is in "boundary created by them" completed the task flawlessly, soon after the event again tiny tots were back to their positions as per the directives.

Just before the event, there was a meeting with the so called high academicians and again Maya was humiliated to the highest notches, but one of the academician who probably, remember her hard work and requested them to be little polite with her as there was no fault on her side.

The humiliation, interrogation continued, she was strictly going as per his commandments, dealing everything with patience, following Gandhigiri, but all the time fighting battle alone was not possible. Maya decided to step down from her position and submitted her resignation by giving a month's notice. The moment her communication was reached to the vice-commander and royal man, there was **tsunami in the establishment.** The Management thought, since Maya was in need of a job and as the responsible, old employee, would stay and continue with the job. Every day she was experiencing some problem which was taking her nearly whole day to prove the correctness of the same. Maya thought atlast she has become a researcher then an administrator. She was happy that if chief would have been there, he would have more than happy to see Maya as a researcher. Every day, for each and every administrative, legal, finance, examination matters, Maya was blamed for the support/legal advice/assistance/correctly performing the duty giving the history to the chief.

The vice-commander called her and said: You have supported the chief, he is an academician and he had secured job in hand and left and rejoin his duties somewhere. He has lot of backing from the city. You are alone, without any support. If you are counting on him, than you are making a mistake, neither he will get you a job nor he will keep communication with you after some time. He has used you as a wall and performed. You will soon realize your mistake. Donot trust that man, I know him very well. You have worked in this establishment for so many years, did anytime we ever doubted your integrity, we know you are with the management. But what has impressed you so much that you are not ready to listen to even management. One day you will approach us for the job because what I am saying, you will agree/ appreciate our perception about that man.

Maya said: I support only to the right and do my duty as professional as the officer of the establishment and in the best interest of the establishment. This is correct because last so many years I have worked for the establishment and not for the person. The vice-commander was taken a back and started thinking about her explanation.

Very next day Maya was again called upon by the vice-commander who insisted that she should give her information on which other committees the chief has been nominated, but Maya did not even gave her slightest hint that he has already been nominated on two national level councils, one is of scientists and another is of education reformers. But her fellow colleagues at the authority bodies are working with all the precautions and without any loophole so that history do not repeat as in the past the chief was nominate on establishment's council and the vice-commander and the royal man/king had made a presentation to the authority and managed to change the composition and chief's name was dropped.

Maya requested the vice-commander to provide the establishment the communication which the chief has written to the authority Committee informing regarding noncompliance of governance system and due to which the establishment has lost the opportunity to come in category of excellent. Maya assured the vice-commander that if such a communication is provided to her than, the establishment could file a case against the chief. How correct Maya was, there was no such communication sent by chief. But was distress, because she was not able to prove innocence of the chief. Though she tried her level best, not because she was supporting chief but she was supporting the truth. By then the vice-commander had informed the members and other stake holders, further blamed the chief publically.

The vice-commander said she has the xerox copy of the communication sent by chief, as the leader of Nation has personally shown her. Maya smiled again that was her cunning smile and requested one copy of the same to be with the establishment's record.

The vice-commander could not answer further, she mentioned to Maya "See for whom you are vouching that crock, stupid, licentious, person has already communicated to the committee about the noncompliance of governance system before the final presentation and none of us knew about the same.

Maya you remember he was very indifferent just before the presentation. But he kept everything to himself, under the carpet. Maya, a very sturdy voice said think how dishonest he was the management was of the opinion that you are aware of the same and supporting his wrong deeds. I assured her that the chief would never do this.

Maya was informed her fellow colleagues from authority that royal man/ king and vice-commander has written communication to the committee against the chief and justifying their stand to file the writ petition and as per the court order the governance system is justified.

She was wondering why the vice-commander is hiding from her the truth knowing well that she too have few fellow colleagues, who will provide me with updates.

Why would chief do such a political act that too when he is leading the establishment. But she did not have any proof to prove that the chief was innocent and was man of principle. Maya could even tell the vice-commander that she have copy of all the communications sent by royal man and the vice-commander, which will prove them guilty and they will lose their prestige in the society and nobody would ever think of admitting their children to such a establishment.

It would be a big scandal where such a well-known, reputed royal man will have to face the public for blaming a scientist and man of repute. But would not reveal the truth, because her fellow colleagues with trust had provided the documents just for her satisfaction and wanted me to know the true colors of royal man and vice-commander. They wanted to publically insult the chief so that his career comes to an end.

But the vice-commander, through sources came to know that Maya is aware of the truth and have all support from her fellow colleagues and capable of reveling the truth publically, decided to get rid of her too, so that truth is wrap and remains the skeleton in the cupboard. The harassment was to its third notches, but she did not give up. It was really battle, was not sure whether will survive or they would do some accident and finish me. But God always take care, the vice-commander was instructed not to harm, this message was communicated to vice-commander by the chairman of the authority committee. He further communicated that if any harm is done to chief or her the management would face consequences. The royal man would be forced to return all the awards he has been bestowed on him.

The Management thought the best way to subdue the matter is to accept her resignation and put the blame on chief. But later doctor, I thought if the truth will be revealed to the world. The world will ever lose the trust / admiration / reverence/high opinion/respect for any teacher and so called academicians. This would be biggest disaster in the learning field.

The very next day, the royal man of the establishment called Maya, he wanted to brief her about the chief, but probably he had other intension, he did not speak anything and was just remained quiet and was trying to read her mind. After about 30 minutes he left. royal man instructed that no leave to be taken during the period of notice. That day she lost her cool and did know as to what to be done. Her mental status was beyond description. Maya called her old friend who was a doctor and told him that I need medical assistance as probably her B.P. was high or low but definitely wanted his help. Maya rushed and got admit herself and took rest. The chief had unique way of sending her rescue operation, sometime through more experience people, sometime friends, sometime other academicians and all the time he was worried about his own people, since he was to leave the battle suddenly.

After two days again she was asked to sign papers which were against her principles and in no circumstance she wanted chief to face be deformation, because he was and is a public figure, scientist, administrator, academician and she never wanted him to get into this dirt politics. Of course the chief would have won the case, but in this small world it was not easy to regain the respect again. The vice-commander knew other than her nobody officially can file the case against the chief. She point blank refused and made them clear that I will/ shall / would not listen anything against the chief, this message was not only to the people working or connected with the establishment but to the entire world. This was her "gift " to him. She till date donot know whether he treats her his follower or not, but it was her "gift" to him. The country is in need of such eminent simple living and high thinking people.

Maya explained to royal man that since the chief has dedicatedly without deviating any rules keeping in mind the principles on which the establishment has been laid and in 18 months' time has taken the establishment to a greater heights. She requested them to relook the progress of the establishment in last decade and also the contributions of the chiefs so far.

There was no answer to her gentle request. But probably after having discussion internally and realized that she will also stand by the truth, she was simply informed that she will not be entitle for any benefits because probably I was not the yes man and they wanted to taste her patience or whether she can be divided. Maya agreed to their offer and gave up all the benefits which was included in gift. She was in total agreement with the commandments of chief and he worked in best interest of establishment and not individual.

She was told, there was literally argument between him and vice-commander. He never wanted her to leave the job. Though to all the new appointees he warns that she is very strict person and doesnot spare any one.

When she again thought, the teacher never wanted his disciple to be more famous, more knowledgeable than himself. These days' people are more for them to become page three personalities or to be in limelight and to sustain that position they go to any extend.

Her witty assistant said: Madam, finally everybody have to stand before the God and give the details of their deeds.

But doctor apart from all the good quality of chief, one quality till date I donot appreciate it. As a colleague if you get something for him to eat or share something which you would prepare for all the colleagues and chief, he use to immediately get angry because probably with the past experience, he never encourage personal things though he did not mean disrespect, he use to feel uncomfortable. Which was not correct, and she always felt that he should not treat everybody in the same square. Probable he has to think on this and do some more research. Only firing or shooting with AK47 sometime doesnot help, people those who respect him feel hurt.

Her witty assistant use to say: Baba (chief) till date never knew how to judge a person.

But that evening, her team was in tears and was proud of their leader. On the same day a confidential report about the chief was asked from the entire employees' community and he got 81 on scale of 100. That was the biggest gift we would give to chief. But nobody could effort to lose their job because they were the bread winner of their respective families. The team were following all his commandments/teaching, but on each and every incidence there was a counter attack on his commandments and the direction in which the establishment was progressing soon came to a languish position.

Next week suddenly, she received the orders from HR stating that her entire team was transferred to different locations. That was the moaning day for the establishment. The team was not even given a hour's notice, it was as if the war has been declared and soldiers immediately deputed to fight out. The team members left their leader by compulsion and proceeded. She was left alone. Many of other officers jokingly said now only the captain is left, one woman army. But she did not wanted to give up and work till the last day of her notice period. Every day the royal man started visiting the establishment and he always wanted her to be there with him till the time he would be in his office. Probably this was another way of harassment to lady.

On the last day of the notice period, it was another episode, the vice-commander called Maya and requested to reconsider the decision but the request was too late. After all the harassment, torched there was no room for reconsideration. Her fellow colleagues were contacted and were requested to have a word with for reconsideration. But she informed them that the facts and mental harassment which I was undergoing.

Maya was waiting with the documents to handing over the charge, but there was not body who could take, finally royal man has to take the charge with a request that for few days this news to be kept under wrap. I agreed to the same and waited for further directives. On the stipulated date I was relived from the duties and became a free bird.

But that was not accepted to the establishment, they tried to contact me again requesting me to come back, guide the Jr. Colleagues. One of her old colleagues mis-leaded the establishment that her own cell phone was provided by the establishment and tried to get the information from the company. But some time law take care of truth and was informed about the most undesirable act. Finally doctor, I have to set the people right at the establishment so that in future the colleagues of mine do not play such immature act.

The Management decided to send the message to chief so that he would instruct me to join back, but soon I came to know about their plan I sounded the chief and he said: they dare not do that....

Maya also observed that the management use to start harassing the will-wishers of chief when he uses to be out of city for conference/official work / personal work etc. Till date I did not understand why they were doing this.

The top leaders in nation and so called the pioneers also could not do much because they all were under the obligation of vice-commander in one way or the other. The only support she received in absence of chief, which one of her fellow colleague came to know the harassment she was undergoing and he immediately wanted me to get some rescue, he informed the highest authority and soon the vice-commander received a communication that she should be spare of harassment. Many of academicians resigned who were appointed by him, the establishment with potential is going to dogs due to false self-imagination of selfish small minds.

Her witty assistant said: What they would gain by harassing people. They should atlesst think about the sincere and honest services that you have given to the establishment.

Many like her hardworking, honest people will be come and work and conditions will not change it will go on and on, because Money and Power can purchase anything in this world. The History will keep repeating but nothing will change.

The chief after handing over the charge as the chief, was actually worried for his army and the leader of mischievous lot. Every day was a challenging day, humiliation was on the agenda item of day to day working. The soldiers were transferred to other boarder areas. The leader was left along, so that one man army could be defeated easily. But the chief did not leave his soldiers; he knew and was very vigilant to provide his army protection, rescue.

Every day, she donot how, doctor by every afternoon the chief's rescue operations with full force were very effective. During the period of battle, the army was in need of emotional/mental support rather than physical support. The chief wanted them to be emotionally very strong and face the situation. every day, well experienced, persons of repute were contacting her, giving her courage, advice, tips and what not. The chief was kept his words of taking care of us.

Dr Louis said but how did she join this kind of establishment, whether she was not aware of the family business, that means she was working with business man and not knowledge providers, when she join this establishment.

Dr Louis was feeling very sorry about her journey of working for so many years, where there were so many difficulties and single handedly bearing, without having any support. He asked me when you started working and where were you prior to 2007.

Dr Louis, said what would be reason behind their uncivilized behavior.

Maya Said; Till today, I fail to understand, why there is no reward for hard work, sincerity and honesty. Doctor said but you should be happy that you had job satisfaction and atleast with proud you can say that you worked honestly otherwise it is difficult to get hardworking willing worker.

Maya said, I realized very late, actually what great people preach they donot practice. It was racisms, the Management wanted to support their own community people rather than other community. But they forget that there is only one religion, humanity. I personally feel if you cannot be a good human being, you cannot understand anything including your professional work. I donot say you should support your own people, but there should be healthy competition.

At end of several years of service, the conclusion was the organizations suck the blood of young energetic, hardworking, willing worker, young people and once the work is complete and they reach to excellence, they withdrawn the staff from their system.

This will continue and nobody will be able to change anything there will be many Maya and each one will face the life in similar or verse than what I faced.

Now again I at square one, looking for the job, requesting royal Men of establishment of repute to give me opportunity, how positive I am when I approach them with request. Everyone just show sympathy but nobody is really concern that a alone lady, with so much of experience and could give the best to their establishment, who believes in principles and honest and dedicated to her work. This is so called world of academician, royal man, truly educated selfish people of repute.

By this time they had already become greedy because of past experience of last two decades. In, it is very easy to put obstacles by approaching the court of law, that is manageable and the authority has so many projects, jobs, policies, ruling, to be attended with meager number of honest officers, how they would take quick /appropriate action. It will be only "date after date" and will take atleast 5-6 years to come to crux of the case and by that time new policy would be ready for implementation. The royal man will remain where he is, the governance system will be same and some honest people would be scarified and lose their jobs. The urge to retain power turns into a cruel game of use and throw. All the possible political, unethical, unscrupulous, methods are used to meet the objective to control by hook or crook. The chief at the end wrote which had tremendous impact on Maya and on demand Maya decided to share "Reflections" sent by chief with every one:

"This day brings joy, happiness and a new beginning to all. On this day we are supposed to transcend the limits of our journey to choose what is virtuous and stretch our abilities to our utmost towards the cause for which we are dedicated.

I joined establishment as the chief. As the higher education system is evolving and rapidly changing in, I hoped that the private establishment like ours could play a leading role. I always believed that n higher education system should have a balanced mix of public and private enterprises so that both mass and class of education remain mutually supportive. At the same time, I trust that education should not remain the preserve of only those who can afford but should be equally available to those who deserve and need it most. I believe that Establishments of excellence can not only be built by strong bricks but more by great minds and committed people. The spirit and philosophy of higher education is a product of team work, leaving no place for personal ego, or compulsion to control others or encouraging sycophancy. I was hoping that at our establishment such a model can be developed where teaching, learning, research, innovation and scholarship is developed by an academic team committed to excellence and not for personal prestige or commercial gain.

I have over 20 years of experience in best n Establishments like as well as in the national institutes like. I was invited to join establishment to help and facilitate for taking the university to a higher level in general and its transition of change in particular to Category A given by the Authority widely known as XXXX Committee. Just for those who may not know this background I must mention that the Authority of had formed this high powered Squad to review and regulate rampant growth and exploitation through commercialization of higher education from many deemed to be Universities. Every University in Category B was put under observation and review to retain their status of a 'establishment'. They were asked to take corrective measures to improve nine parameters covering the basic questions ranging from the 'Idea of a establishment' to academic innovations, research output, quality of Faculty, compliance to Authority regulations and most importantly the governance system. The message from the Authority was loud and clear that the establishment must be similar or be better in all respects to other Universities and should not function merely as successful business models or simply remain as undergraduate teaching institutes or colleges. This distinction must be clearly demonstrated by presence of eminent research intensive faculty, high quality publications, intellectual property, knowledge development, scholarship and innovations. This was a colossal task and grand challenge as it involved issues related to capacity building and mindset changes in the whole ecosystem. Importantly, the regulations also required reducing or minimizing exclusive family control in governance for their public credibility, accountability and transparency.

To address this challenge, her strategy as chief was simple - attract best talents, create vibrant grounds for meeting great minds, creating ideas, inspire faculty and students to embrace research, innovation and entrepreneurship. Her strategy was to inculcate and strengthen research as a culture right from the under graduate level. Apart from some „blue sky research", there must also be some social relevance and environmental sensitivity. Research should not to be seen in isolation for the purpose of getting notches qualifications like PhDs. The students and the faculty should have a 'Passion' for learning. Above all, we must produce students who think as well as have skills for problem solving to emerge as socially and globally responsible citizens. I thought it important to give academic freedom without compromising the rigor and encourage confluence of interdisciplinary faculties likes technology and biomedicine; information technology, management and behavioural sciences are just few examples, which I experimented at SIU. Initially it was possible for me to take rapid initiative to change the prevailing state of affairs especially because of the general pressure from the Authority and the XXX Committee.

Thus, within a relatively short span, I could recruit over 150 teaching Faculty; established new Chair Professorships, started new disciplines like Liberal Arts, Biomedical Sciences; restructured and strengthened research programs, introduced new integrated MBA-PhD, MSc-PhD, M.Tech-PhD programs with 50 research Fellowships from University funds, established Research Innovation Council Chaired by eminent personality, established three strategic research clusters in engineering, biomedical sciences, humanities along with high level scientific advisory committees, attempted to restructure Board of Management and Academic Council with eminent people established high power committee to 'revisit programmes. Through special efforts I invited reputed Councils to become recognized research centers. I conceptualized and facilitated publication of 'Natures wonders at

Symbiosis' – a unique publication covering over 200 plant species. I ensured monthly meetings of Leadership team, encouraged ideas like weekly Faculty Club and engaged with them to open minds to promote inter and intra establishment for collaborations. I also tried to streamline the work of BoS, AC and other bodies towards academic excellence including development of benchmarking performance of various Faculties. A prestigious grant from a reputed company to two of the institutes is just one of the many examples of significant outcomes. I received overwhelming response from the entire academic fraternity of the University

Soon however, the picture altered perceptibly. The required reforms in governance crucially needed for real progress were not forth coming as the founder and his family members were unable or unwilling to part with their total control over all policy and operational activities. Worse, the interference in the day to day management of the Establishmentonly increased. The already deep rooted loyalty and sycophancy trait surfaced at every step. The true face of governance, its motives and colors started becoming ominously clear. One major incidence that may have triggered the turn of events must be mentioned here. While the establishment had given an undertaking to the Authority that it will adopt and follow the new Regulations in letters and spirit, the Management suddenly decided to challenge them in the Court. This was probably to enable the royal man to continue as a lifelong chief of chief of the establishment. As chief I did record her dissent and tried hard to persuade Board to refrain from taking such detrimental step, which was against the interest of the establishment. Few eminent members of repute also recorded their dissents; however, the resolution was passed by simple majority by the Board. Obviously the family interests prevailed over the University and as a result, as of it stands today, the fate of the University remains unknown although most of the academic parameters were complied with and presented to the taskforce in a satisfactory manner by me. I am of the opinion that unless and until the governance structure of the Establishments is totally made independent of the sponsoring Society and professionally function as envisaged by the new Regulations in letter and spirit, the fate of Establishmentis bound to remain uncertain. Many Establishments taking recourse to judiciary itself speaks for desperate attempts to retain total power and control by the founding family."

It came to her *notice that other Establishments have been placed in Category A by the Authority but the decision of our establishment was apparently withheld. The Authority reclassification was very crucial for the very existence of the establishment and its future growth, which was seriously compromised because of deficiencies in governance system and Society's forced decision on the establishment to challenge new Regulations. After I learned about the Authority decision of withholding reclassification of our establishment, same day, I decided to exit from her assignment in a dignified fashion and submitted her resignation as chief, which was accepted by the royal man.*

Personally, I respect royal man, both as her teacher and creator of such a big empire, however, I do not agree with his views that the public Trust or a registered Society could be treated as a family property or administered as a proprietorship. A recent judgment of High Court indicate that once a Trust is established, the role of Founders is only of a Trustee and not as a Proprietor and it cannot be treated as a property of any family. I sincerely believe that it is possible to run a Private Establishmentsuccessfully, based on the good governance and professionalism as exemplified few others. In the sum, I could not accept ad hoc and autocratic governance with consistent direct interference by the Management representatives. It seems to me that according to them the role of a chief in reality was merely to be a showpiece and a rubberstamp – and I refused to degrade myself to either. As a result, when I was not successful to persuade Founder through several letters and discussions to adopt good governance practices and financial discipline, in line with the new Regulations, I thought it is best to step down instead of struggling to do duty or to carry out work in marginalized and hostile surroundings.

When I look back, I feel good and grateful that many thought leaders, distinguished academicians, educationists and media from and abroad have appreciated his efforts to take establishment to greater heights. I thank them all. While accepting his *resignation even royal man has placed on record his appreciation for the valuable services rendered by me and also for* his *efforts in enhancing the reputation of establishment. I appreciate this parting gesture. While working at establishment, I have also come across, appreciated and encouraged some academicians of great potential, who I have no doubt, will distinguish themselves in future given the right environment. I wish them all the best.*

All life, due to family upbringing and training, I have always worked honestly and diligently in the best interest of the establishment but not in the interest of any individual. I have always taken a principled stand, listened to her 'inner voice' and have never compromised on values and moral obligations to the establishment as also to the society. I wish to take this opportunity to thank all her mentors and friends like you for their guidance during this ordeal and look forward for your continued support.

Her witty assistant said: why the chief did not inform us, finally he also deceived us. This time Maya had no answer for her witty assistant.

Dr Louis was pained hear Maya he was thinking that what a mind-gripping tale, the readers will find a reflection of the society and the life as they see it. They will smile, frown and they will be surely taken by surprise. Surprise at the extent to which a system can be modified and corrupted to suit individual needs. Surprise at the delusions people call life. Surprise at to what level a mighty individual stoops to cover up his crimes.

All the same, it is not a read-today-forget-tomorrow story. This narrative seethes with questions about the system that shapes our lives day in and out. What is more important, the reader will find himself asking questions, akin to the ones Maya faces here while going through her administrative duties, unaware of the hurdles in her path.

Till date Maya is without job, the chief has forgotten her, her sacrifice, honesty, sincerity dedication because nobody has time or ready to help Maya, this is probably most intense shock Maya had.

Maya is still has hope that she will get good job probably this illusion, because now it all most 2 years she has no job.

Printed in the United States
By Bookmasters